Are You Frustrated Wi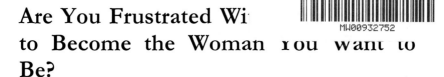 to Become the Woman Iou want to Be?

If you've struggled to end destructive habits and maintain healthy ones...
If you've wondered how other women seem to balance it all...
If you want more peace, love, and joy...

You need to be Wonder Woman! Extraordinary living is possible – not with the Secret – but with the Super Power. Are you ready to be transformed?

SO YOU'RE NOT WONDER WOMAN?
How Your Super Power Can Change Your Life

Scripture taken from the HOLY BIBLE, NEW INTERNATIONAL VERSION®. NIV®. Copyright© 1973, 1978, 1984 by International Bible Society. Used by permission of Zondervan. All rights reserved.

For further information, contact the publisher: CreateSpace Publishing, www.createspace.com

The author has made every diligent effort to ensure that the information in this book is accurate and complete. She assumes no responsibility for errors or omissions that are inadvertent or inaccurate.

ISBN: 1434805085

SO YOU'RE NOT WONDER WOMAN?

How Your Super Power Can Change Your Life

Melanie Wilson, Ph.D.

CreateSpace Publishing
www.createspace.com

This book is dedicated to my mother, LuAnne.
Without you, I wouldn't be Wonder Woman!

Contents

Acknowledgements

I am listed as the author, but many people are responsible for this book:

Gail Swenson, my high school English teacher. You always believed I'd be an author. Now I am!

My husband, my Superman. Thank you for putting up with Melanie and being my best friend, my agent, my publisher, and the source of my best material. Most of all, thank you for never letting me forget who I am.

My children. Thank you for understanding when Mommy has to write and speak and for your interest in everything I do. I'm so blessed to enjoy six Incredible kids every day!

My family. Thank you for your faith, love, and support. Thank you Nancy for forging the self-publishing trail for me!

Deena. If not for your encouragement to self-publish, this book would still be in my head.

Phyllis. Thank you seems too small for your mentoring, friendship, and editing, but you like it concise!

Deb. Your belief in me and prayers on my behalf have been invaluable. I'm proud to be in a league with you!

Wendy. Your "edgy" life story has given me the courage to share mine.

Debbie and Shannon. Thank you for the friendship and the fun. You are true Wonder Sisters.

Moms of 3 boys. Your ever-present online "ear" has blessed me beyond measure.

Laura. Though you knew Melanie quite well, you've always treated me like Wonder Woman.

Marla. I've learned to FLY by fluttering after you. Thanks for the wings!

The late Mark Spitz. I'm grateful for your writing instruction: not how or what, but for whom.

Women I've met and counseled. I am particularly indebted to the woman who wished my talk, "So You're Not Wonder Woman?" was in book form. This book is for all of you and the Wonder Women you love.

The Super Power. You wrote this book on the pages of my life and it has been my joy and privilege to put the words on paper. Thank you for loving me enough to make me Wonder Woman.

Introduction

From the planning stage for this book, I have been plagued by guilt and doubt about Melanie Wilson's worthiness as its author. Melanie seems to have all the right qualifications. At one time, she lived with legions of roach roommates, stacks of dirty dishes and bags of moldy laundry. She constantly forgot appointments, procrastinated important tasks, and wrote checks until they bounced. She couldn't stop eating, couldn't start exercising, and wouldn't end emotionally abusive relationships. Melanie was a mess!

Eventually, Melanie moved from the roach motel and into a decent apartment. She met and married a faithful man, lost weight, and found a system for keeping her home organized. The life change was so dramatic that Melanie wrote about it. Her article on getting organized FLYLady-style was published in *Woman's Day* magazine. She was even interviewed for radio, newspapers, and television on the subject.

Melanie certainly looks the part of the life-change expert. She has a Ph.D. in psychology, homeschools six children, coordinates ministries and charity events, writes, speaks, and still manages to find time to go on dates with her husband and enjoy several hobbies.

But the truth is, Melanie Wilson hasn't changed and she never will. Many days she doesn't practice what she preaches. She doesn't make her bed, shine her sink, or prepare for the next day. Melanie once spent two frantic hours trying to find the location of her speaking engagement because she hadn't written it down. She was speaking on getting organized!

One night Melanie was up late and didn't check her calendar for the next day's activities. She assumed she could sleep in. A startling phone call the next morning from Phyllis Wallace of the "Woman to Woman" radio program reminded her she was lined up for an in-studio interview with former Miss America, Debbye Turner!

You probably understand why I could not in good conscience allow Melanie to write this book. I, Wonder Woman, will be writing it instead. If you identify with Melanie's struggle to make significant, lasting change, the following pages offer you hope.

There is hope for you if:

- ✓ Your house is such a mess that you begin to hyperventilate at the thought of unannounced guests

- ✓ Your New Year's resolution is the same year after year

✓ One or more of your relationships is making you miserable

✓ You feel like life is out of control

✓ You're not the patient, firm, devoted mother you want to be

✓ You think you lack the willpower gene

✓ You forget things so often your organized friends give you reminders without being asked

✓ You know you are your own worst enemy

✓ Life feels vaguely empty

✓ You've tried to change before and here you are…

Whether change is absolutely necessary for you or would just be nice, I have some good news! Change *is* possible. You simply have to become the heroine you were created to be: Wonder Woman.

If you're like most women, the thought of becoming Wonder Woman is laughable. You may think I'm joking or that the crazy psychologist stereotype is true after all. I assure you I am not making this up. I'm serious. I believe I am Wonder Woman and that you can be, too.

In the pages ahead, I hope to convince you of your true identity, encourage you to put on your Wonder Woman suit, and show you how your Super Power can change your life for good.

HOW TO USE THIS BOOK

When I read a book like this one, I often ignore any
practical applications until I've read it all. When I want to go
back and apply what I've learned, I have a hard time
relocating the exercises. If you read like I do, you will
appreciate having all the applications at the back of the
book. The Wonder Woman Workouts are exercises to help
bring about the changes you long for.

You can benefit from reading this book as an individual,
but reading it as part of a book club or Bible study could be
even more powerful. We all know maintaining an exercise
routine is more successful with a friend. Which of your
friends is ready for a change? Why don't you email or call
her now? If you're well acquainted with the Super Power,
please share this book with someone who isn't. I've written
it especially for her.

Wonder Years

"We need a renaissance of wonder. We need to renew, in our hearts and in our souls, the deathless dream, the eternal poetry, the perennial sense that life is miracle and magic."

E. *Merrill Root*

Once upon a time, I knew I was a wonder. Then I forgot.

I was raised in farm country. Isn't every good superhero? When I was growing up, my mama told me I could do anything and I believed her. My dreams were as big as the night sky over my head and I knew they would come true. I was the girl who sang loud and raised my hand in class and wanted to be somebody. I didn't know whether I'd be a teacher, doctor, actress, lawyer, hairdresser, writer, or singer, but I knew my life was going to be an exciting adventure. I knew that I was special and beautiful and that I had a purpose on this earth. I knew I was Wonder Girl.

As I grew, my teachers recognized me, but criticized other children if they weren't as wonderful. Instead of being thrilled by my special calling, my peers resented me. They didn't call me Wonder Girl; they called me Teacher's Pet. They refused to play with me, ridiculed my clothing and appearance and attacked me physically. I was hit with books, lunch boxes, and fists. When the teacher left the classroom one afternoon, my desk was overturned and my fingers and belongings were stomped on as I tried to right myself. At home, my mom continued to tell me who I was, but I began to wish I weren't such a wonder.

I tried to hide my good grades and I bought new clothes. I quit raising my hand so much and tried to make friends with bullies by being as nice as I could be. It didn't work. The rejection was so painful I decided to try living like a mere mortal. Melanie took over more of my life and I found that kids liked her better.

When I started high school, my English teacher reminded me who I really was. Like my mom, she told me I could be anything and do anything. I was scared, but I decided to live as Wonder Woman at least some of the time. I was pleased to discover most of my peers had matured enough by then that they didn't mind. I poured myself into wonderful challenges: acting, singing, writing, speaking, running, softball and class leadership.

I felt liberated, but I wasn't entirely accepted. When I found myself really flying, someone I cared about would tell me I looked ridiculous. I was doing too much, they said. I needed to slow down. So I'd come back to earth and be plain ole Melanie again.

As a college student, I found a few opportunities to be my super heroine self, but it was obvious that people continued to prefer ordinary. I tried to be good, but not great. Greatness continued to result in painful rejection. I applied to graduate school with only a glimmer of my true identity left. I allowed myself to daydream about becoming the surgeon general. I imagined joining the military and once

I had the appointment, I would travel the country speaking to Americans about good mental and physical health. When people laughed, I realized I was aiming too high. I decided to become a health psychologist instead and everyone seemed to approve.

Once in graduate school, I learned I had been brainwashed into my supernatural way of thinking. I had been sheltered from the real world. In the real world, there was no Wonder Woman. She was a girlish fantasy and I had grown up.

Who Do You Think You Are?

You succeed by finding ways to capitalize on who you are, not by trying to fix who you aren't.

First, Break All the Rules

You may be wondering if this is some kind of crazy Sybil story. Or maybe you think I'm arrogant, claiming to be Wonder Woman. If you didn't feel like Wonder Girl growing up, I can understand that reaction. Maybe you never felt beautiful. Maybe you didn't get good grades. Maybe you didn't participate in many activities. Maybe you didn't discover a particular talent. So maybe you're not Wonder Woman after all?

I didn't remember I was Wonder Woman until I was a homeschooling mother of three. I'd just discovered how to FLY and keep my home in order (we'll discuss flight training later). My friend had recently had a baby, so I made meals for my family and hers, wrapped up gifts for the new baby and his siblings, and drove to her home. While at my friend's home, I held the baby, chatted with my friend, and discussed the virtues of homeschooling with my friend's husband. When it was time for me to leave, my friend's husband held the door open for me as I ran to my car in the rain. "Bye, Wonder Woman!" he called after me.

I laughed all the way home. "Wonder Woman!" Ha, ha, ha! I was Wonder Woman? How funny! But something about being called Wonder Woman unlocked the door to an old dream. I was like an amnesia patient remembering who I was. Suddenly, I realized I had been created to live life to the full. I wasn't supposed to be defeated by disorganization, disobedient kids or a cranky husband. I was equipped to overcome adversity and stand for truth, justice, and the American way! I was supposed to be somebody. I was Wonder Woman!

When I got home, I called my best friend and told her I had my memory back. Then I told her she was Wonder Woman, too. She said, "Yeah, well *you* are, but I'm not." I said, "Yes, you are *too* Wonder Woman" and we did the "No I'm not; yes you are" thing for a while until finally from deep within her came a little girl giggle that I hadn't heard in years. I screeched, "See? You know you are!"

You see, my Wonder Sister, I know you are, too. I don't care if you're model thin or far past pleasingly plump. I don't care if you're a Mensa member or a high school dropout. And I don't care if everyone you've ever known has told you you're a no-good loser. I know you were created to be Wonder Woman.

OUR FAMILY HISTORY

How do I know you're my Wonder Sister? Allow me to give you our family history.

If you're familiar with the Wonder Woman of comics and television, you may have heard that we are descendants of an immortal Amazon princess. She was a woman made out of clay and brought to life by the breath of a god. She lived on Paradise Island and was blessed with supernatural strength and armor that protected her.

Story has it that Wonder Woman fell in love with a mortal named Steve Trevor. He was a U.S. Army Intelligence agent who was wounded when he crashed his plane near Paradise Island. Wonder Woman cared for him and brought him to an Army hospital in the States.

When Wonder Woman learned Steve had recovered, she needed to find a way to stay close to him. She met an Army nurse named Diana Prince who was weeping at the entrance to the hospital. Wonder Woman noticed the marked resemblance between herself and Diana. She learned that Diana was distressed because her fiancé had been transferred across the country. Wonder Woman struck a deal with Diana that enabled Diana to move on and allowed her to assume Diana's identity.

I love fairy tales, but I love amazing true stories even more. The Wonder Woman you're most familiar with is a fairy tale. I love the idea there's a woman who is strong, beautiful, capable, conquering, and self-sacrificing, don't you? But the true story of Wonder Woman is even more captivating.

Our real history is recorded in a book written thousands of years ago. The first Wonder Woman, like the comic book version, was immortal. She was created from clay and the creator God breathed life into her. She was placed in Paradise to live forever. She was strong and beautiful, but had no need of armor, for she, and the garden she lived in, were perfect.

Her life source and creator – her Super Power – gave her everything she needed for life and happiness, but He also gave her one rule. She was not to eat from a certain tree in the garden. Eating the fruit of that tree would separate her from her Super Power and would end in death.

Foolishly, she listened to the Super Power's enemy, the lying serpent, and ate the forbidden fruit. The serpent convinced her she needed something more than God had given her to be perfect. That fruit tasted so good and the serpent was right – she hadn't died! She gave it to her Superman and he ate some, too. It didn't take our Wonder Woman ancestor long to figure out that although the fruit tasted good, it was rotten to the core. Once she had known only joy, self-confidence, and freedom; now she knew shame, fear, and powerlessness.

The Super Power drove Wonder Woman and Superman out of Paradise, but promised that one day a true Superhero would save them. While they waited, the two found that they inhabited bodies of death. They were now mortal.

YOU'VE GOT THE WRONG WOMAN

Perhaps you know this story and can't imagine how you, an ordinary woman, can be Wonder Woman. When the Super Power, God, created Wonder Woman, He said she was good (Genesis 1). Even after her disobedience and the disobedience of every woman after her, one of the great heroes of our history is recorded as saying to God, "I praise you because I am fearfully and wonderfully made; your works are wonderful, I know that full well" (Psalm 139:14). We are full of the wonders of God! That makes us Wonder Women.

Ravi Zacharias wrote of the wonders that we are in his newsletter, *Just Thinking*.[1] In describing a presentation by Francis Collins, the director of the Human Genome Project, he wrote:

In his last slide, he showed two pictures side by side. On the left appeared a magnificent photo of the stained-glass rose window from Yorkminster Cathedral in Yorkshire, England, its symmetry radiating from the center, its colors and geometric patterns spectacular—clearly a work of art purposefully designed by a gifted artist. Its sheer beauty stirred the mind. On the right side of the screen appeared a slide showing a cross section of a strand of human DNA. The picture did more than take away one's breath; it was awesome in the profoundest sense of the term—not just beautiful, but overwhelming. And it almost mirrored the pattern of the rose window in Yorkminster...The audience gasped at the sight, for it saw itself. The design, the color, the splendor of the design left everyone speechless...

We may not like what we see in the mirror every morning, but we are wonders to behold because we were made in the very image of God (Genesis 1:26).

Still not convinced you are Wonder Woman? There are three reasons we have a case of amnesia when it comes to knowing who we really are.

PERFECTABLE, NOT PERFECT

The first reason our identity is in question is because we've believed that we have to be perfect to be Wonder Woman. If a vote were taken for just one "perfect" woman, Mary, the mother of Jesus, would likely win the title. Though she was a true Wonder Woman – as beautiful as a stained glass window – Joanna Weaver writes:

> Tradition tells us that when some ancient artisans portrayed Mary in stained glass, they used clear material. No dyes, no colors, just transparent-as-water glass. The reason was that, when Mary offered herself to God, she offered herself unreservedly and completely. "There was nothing of her to affect the light that came through," says pastor and author Ben Patterson.[2]

The truth is Mary was not perfect and neither are we (Romans 3:23). The first Wonder Woman *was* perfect, however, and so was her home. She enjoyed a close friendship with a perfect Super Power. But once she disobeyed, she was like a beautiful stained glass window with a crack in it. Every time she did something out of pride or selfishness, the crack grew. Eventually, her life was left in shattered pieces. She tried to pick up the pieces of her own life, but got hurt in the process.

The Super Power loved Wonder Woman, though she was no longer perfect. He saw that no matter how hard she tried, she couldn't put the window of her life back together. There was only one thing He could do: He sent His Son to save her.

The Son was born of an imperfect woman named Mary, conceived by the perfect Holy Spirit, and raised by an imperfect carpenter named Joseph. The Son was the perfect man for the job because He was the original creator of the Wonder Woman masterpiece. He picked up the pieces and made the window new. As He did, every broken piece of her life cut Him. His blood was all over her, washing away the dirt that had accumulated. He sacrificed His own life, so she might have hers to the full.

Now when the Super Power sees His Wonder Woman, He sees a beautiful stained glass window with His light shining through. Is she perfect? No. If we look closely, we can see the marks of a broken life. But God doesn't see those. Instead, He sees the perfect blood that stains her.

When I was a girl, I thought Lynda Carter was the perfect Wonder Woman. For starters, the Lynda-Carter Wonder Woman was absolutely gorgeous. She also seemed to have the perfect balance of kindness, goodness, and self-control on TV. She would be firm with the crooks, but not overly mean. Even though she was so Wonder-full, she wasn't self-centered. If that's not perfect, what is?

On discussing her role as Wonder Woman, Lynda Carter said, "I tried to play her like a regular woman who just happened to have superhuman powers." Lynda Carter did us Wonder Women proud. She played us as we really are:

regular, imperfect women who just happen to have a perfect Super Power.

STRIVING, NOT STRESSED

A second reason we don't know who we are is everyone tells us we're not Wonder Women. Well-meaning teachers of organization and time-management skills tell us that believing we are Wonder Women is prideful perfectionism – the source of all our stress. In *I'm Not Wonder Woman, but God Made Me Wonderful,* Sheila Walsh gently suggests that we take off our wrinkled Wonder Woman suits and put them away if we want more peace and joy. I think Ms. Walsh and I agree in principle, but I disagree that the source of our distress is raising the bar too high. I believe we have set it far too low. When our Super Power created the first Wonder Woman, He didn't say:

"Be careful not to do too much."
"You're only human."
"You have to take care of *you.*"

Can you imagine Lynda Carter's Wonder Woman saying, "I'd love to help you stop this crime, but my counselor has advised me that I need to learn to say 'no' and take care of me?" Wonder Woman wasn't given superpowers to take care of Lynda; she was given power to serve others.

Even after our ancestor's disastrous disobedience, the Super Power didn't discourage aspiring super heroes. On the contrary, His words to us are:

I tell you the truth, if you have faith as small as a mustard seed, you can say to this mountain, 'Move from here to there' and it will move. Nothing will be impossible for you (Matthew 17:20).

I tell you the truth, anyone who has faith in me will do what I have been doing. He will do even greater things than these (John 14:12a).

The Apostle Paul, a leader in the early Christian church, accuses some of its members of behaving like mere mortals (1 Corinthians 3:3). He also says, "Do you not know that in a race all the runners run, but only one gets the prize? Run in such a way as to get the prize" (1 Corinthians 9:24). Clearly we are expected to be extraordinary!

Our history book, the Bible, is full of many true stories of superheroes like you and me. There is the story of a man named Samson with super human strength (Judges 13-16). David was a boy who defeated a giant with only a slingshot (1 Samuel 17). Elijah outran a chariot in the midst of a storm (1 Kings 18:46). Esther saved the lives of her people using superhuman wisdom (Esther).

All of the experts who encourage us not to reach for greatness mean well. After all, there are risks involved. The fairy tale Wonder Woman often gets tied up by her enemies. We Wonder Women can end up tied in knots, too. I often share in seminars on getting organized Wonder-Woman style that we were not meant to be defeated simply for lack of organization! Yet we so often stay bound in our own rope, refusing to draw on the power for change that would release us. Then we wonder why life feels so monotonous.

John and Stasi Eldredge, authors of *Captivating*, write that as women we were created with a desire to participate in a great adventure. Wonder Woman was not created for bondage, but for the freedom to serve. Can you picture what would happen if Sacajawea asked her counselor whether or not she should be part of the Lewis and Clark expedition?

> "Oh Sacajawea, you'll get yourself killed. Someone else can do it. It's like you think you can't be replaced on this mission."

We are not only told to play it safe; we're told we're dispensable. Plenty of other people can do what we do, we hear. Yet when the fairy tale Wonder Woman was in bondage, no other heroine flew to the rescue. Sacajawea was one-of-a-kind and my Wonder Sister, there is no one else in the world like you. Though the Super Power can manage each great expedition without us, He gives us the desire of our hearts by allowing us to play a vital role.

DEAD BUT NOT DONE AWAY WITH

The third reason we have forgotten our true identity is our split personality. The fairy tale Wonder Woman isn't always a super-heroine. Sometimes she is Diana Prince, army nurse. Sometimes I am not Wonder Woman; I'm Melanie Wilson, wife and mother. The fairy tale Wonder Woman didn't have much trouble dealing with her split personality, but I do!

I'm going to put the personality problem in fairy tale terms. We are each like a princess who's eaten a poison apple. (Remember the first Wonder Woman?) In essence, we are dead and unable to save ourselves, though we don't know it. We are much like Cole in the movie, *The Sixth Sense*, who doesn't realize he is seeing dead people because he himself is dead. Unless we are kissed by the Prince, we will remain dead. A terrible dragon does everything possible to keep us from the Prince's kiss. Once awakened to this great love, however, we will live happily ever after. But there's a twist. We ride off into the sunset with some extra baggage: our old dead self.

In the comedy, *National Lampoon's Vacation*, the Griswold family is forced to make room for a relative's dead body on their road trip. Aunt Edna was annoying when she was alive, but really gets on everyone's nerves once she is dead.

The Bible tells us when we trust in the Prince to save us, our old self is dead (Romans 6:6). Like Aunt Edna, our old self is annoying. She's the one who eats poisoned apples when she knows she shouldn't. She's the one who's never satisfied. She's the one who's powerless to change. When she is dead, we are enabled to live as Wonder Women. We have the power to lead changed lives. But we still have to deal with an annoying dead body.

In *Death Becomes Her*, Meryl Streep's and Goldie Hawn's characters go to great lengths to cover up the fact that they are dead. When we think we're good enough the way we are or when we try to change ourselves, we're living like walking corpses. Only the Super Power, who brought His Son Jesus back to life after death on a cross, can give us new lives as Wonder Women. Although we have a new life with the Prince, we're still haunted by our old, dead selves.

Author Joanna Weaver calls her old, dead self "Flesh Woman."[3] Author and speaker Pam Young, calls her old self her "inner brat."[4] She's named her brat Nellie after the queen of all brats from the "Little House on the Prairie" television series. Her Nellie behaves like a typical brat, says Pam, demanding what she wants, when she wants it, regardless of how it affects others.

The greatest human hero of the Christian faith is arguably Paul, author of much of the Bible's New Testament. Despite the many miracles associated with Paul, he proclaimed:

> I know that nothing good lives in me, that is, in my sinful nature. For I have the desire to do what is good, but I cannot carry it out. For what I do is not the good I want to do; no, the evil I do not want to do—this I keep on doing (Romans 7:18-19).

Apparently, Paul had an inner brat, too! I call my fleshy, bratty, old, dead self "Melanie." Whatever you call yours, she's probably called you and said:

"I don't want to clean. We can do it tomorrow."
"Exercise is booooooring. Let's watch TV instead."
"I want chocolate. We deserve it!"
"Can we be done now? "

Our old self is one reason we struggle to make positive, lasting change. But don't despair! Although Nellie's character was never eliminated from the "Little House on the Prairie" show, she was usually put in her place. The Prince will not only save us, but will give us wisdom for putting our annoying "roommate" in her place, too. We'll talk about how to do just that in the pages ahead.

My sister-in-law and I were recently talking with a troubled young woman about the Super Power's ability to change her life. The young lady sheepishly told us that her apartment was such a mess that she couldn't find the papers she needed for her college classes. She admitted she was also doing "stupid stuff with boys." When my sister-in-law asked her what she meant by "stupid stuff," she gave us a look that said, "I'm afraid to say for fear of what you'll think of me."

I could guess what she was thinking. She could see that I was Wonder Woman, the straight-laced mother of six who'd done no wrong. Then I told her about Melanie and she wasn't afraid to be real anymore. We talked openly about the destructiveness of sex with jerks, the crippling effect of slovenly living, and how the Super Power could change it all.

Before we go any further, I think you need to know the truth about Melanie, too. Your old self may look squeaky clean next to Melanie. Maybe you'll feel a lot better about your old gal! Or you may wish you had it so good, because life with your old self has been really, *really* bad. You may see parts of the old you in the old me. Whatever your perspective, I hope you are encouraged. Know this: Melanie and your old self don't star in the show. Wonder Woman does!

Wayward Years

Of all human ills, greatest is fortune's wayward tyranny.

Sophocles, *Ajax*

Even though she wasn't completely beloved, Wonder Girl had been a star – someone to look up to. Now that Melanie was a grown-up, she reasoned that princesses and twinkling stars were the stuff of fairy tales. She exchanged her dream castle for a dump and Prince Charming for a couple of chumps. She started with "Once upon a time," but gave up on "happily ever after."

ROACH MOTEL

For the first time in Melanie's life, she was living alone – or so she thought. She noticed she had a few bugs in her apartment. She thought they were water bugs. They seemed to really enjoy water. Whenever Melanie washed dishes, they would run down the faucet and jump into the sink. That made dish washing rather difficult. She had never seen a roach before, maybe because the weather in her home state of South Dakota was too cold for them.

By the time Melanie figured out her roommates were roaches, her apartment was infested with them. She had no idea that her habit of leaving dirty dishes in the sink and garbage in the can at night was spawning a population explosion. Before she knew it, she was unable to open a kitchen cabinet or even a desk drawer without screaming. The bugs and their eggs were everywhere. At night, they crawled all over her bed. It was like being on *Fear Factor* with no prize money.

She was afraid to ask her landlord for help, for fear she'd be evicted. Melanie tried to evict her roommates herself. At times, she would gamely try to remove them from her cabinets, armed with insecticide. Other times, she set traps. When neither of these approaches worked, she set a bomb – an insecticide bomb. But no matter what she tried, the roaches refused to leave. So she did.

Melanie spent less and less time in her apartment. She gladly accepted occasional invitations to sleep in her girlfriend's bug-free apartment. She spent most of the rest of her time on campus.

When Melanie did return to her apartment, she didn't spend time doing laundry. The washer and dryer were in the basement and her apartment was on the second floor. She was usually too tired to be hassled with doing it. She kept her dirty clothes in the basement until she "had time" to wash them. One morning when she was prepared to get caught up, she discovered that the basement had flooded. Her clothing was moldy and ruined. That wasn't the only part of Melanie's life that stunk.

LAB EXPERIMENT

Melanie enrolled in graduate school to learn about psychopathology. She wanted to understand what was wrong with people and how to fix them. Her apartment served as a living lab experiment for a budding psychologist.

Melanie made the mistake of telling one of the men in her apartment building that she was studying psychology. He called her one night and asked her to drive to another town, 20 miles away, to buy him some cigarettes. When she refused, he said, "I'm drunk and if you don't do it, I'll drive. If I kill someone, it'll be your fault." Thankfully, Melanie convinced her neighbor to wait to buy cigarettes until he was sober.

Melanie was home sick with the stomach flu one day and received another call from her resident drunk. He asked, "Can you come over and talk to me and my buddy? We're both alcoholics and we need help." When Melanie explained she was sick, she was told she could certainly take a couple of hours to recover before she came over to counsel them. Melanie decided she didn't want to work with alcoholics even when she was over the flu.

Melanie was afraid to see her alcoholic neighbor, but she was even more afraid of the neighbor on the other side of her. The walls weren't insulated and her door appeared to be made of cardboard. She could frequently hear a man shouting and throwing things and a woman shouting back. Sometimes it sounded like the man was hitting her. Melanie didn't know what to do. Was she supposed to call the police? If she did, would the man punch his arm through her cardboard door and hurt her too? She just covered her ears and tried to sleep.

The phone rang one afternoon and the caller was a man she didn't recognize. The man said he had seen her and wanted to know if she had a boyfriend. She said she did, hoping the man would no longer be interested. The man said he didn't care that she had a boyfriend. "We can just have an affair and no one will be the wiser," he implored. Melanie assured him that she would not be having an affair with someone she'd never even met and the conversation ended. But the calls didn't.

The mystery man seemed harmless at first, even a little amusing. But the continuing phone calls and cryptic notes scared Melanie. The man made it clear he was watching her. When she went to her car in the mornings, there was often a note from him, encouraging her to give him a chance. Melanie determined that her mystery man/stalker was living in her apartment building. She had no idea if he was just annoying or really dangerous. All she was learning in graduate school was how to conduct research and compute statistics! What she needed was a class on defending herself from alcoholics, batterers, and stalkers.

HEARTBREAK HOTEL

When Melanie arrived in a new town to begin her graduate studies, she was too much in love to worry about a stalker. Shortly before her move, she had ended a rocky, long-term relationship that had begun in high school and started a new, more mature relationship. The new guy had a great job and a great car. He lived ten hours away, but he'd said the "L" word. Melanie figured it was only a matter of time before they solved the distance dilemma. Turns out she was right.

Just a few weeks into her studies, Mr. Mature called and said he had to break up with Melanie because she didn't fit with his career plans. When Melanie expressed her feelings of shock and sadness, he told her she should be thinking about how hard this was for *him*. When the phone call ended, she'd never felt more alone.

Melanie had hoped she would be married or would at least have a serious relationship by the time she finished college. Instead, she found herself in graduate school with no prospects. Meeting someone other than a stalker became a top priority.

Meeting someone meant going to clubs. One weekend at a dance club, she met a factory worker. She had absolutely nothing in common with him, but when he told Melanie his father had recently died of a brain tumor, she gave him her number out of sympathy.

Dance Club Man called the next day and dinner and a movie were planned for the following weekend. He arrived on time, but knocked on the door to the apartment complex, rather than her apartment door. Because of the thin walls, she could hear him knocking below. She hoped if she ignored his knocking, he might go away. He didn't. He eventually determined that he must come inside the building.

He arrived bearing a basket of daisies with an empty card holder. Melanie had to wait for him to remove the pile of trash from his front seat before she could get into his car.

Once seated, her date was careful to turn on his Fuzz Buster. She said, "Oh, are we late for dinner?"

At the restaurant, Melanie's date made conversation. He wanted to know what Melanie liked to do for fun. She talked about her hobbies and he shared his. "I like to drive fast along the shoulder of the road." Melanie wasn't sure he was serious. Then he spoke seriously with her about his past relationships.

"What I don't understand is why women are always afraid of me. Sure, I've broken down some doors and smashed some furniture, but I've never hit anyone," he told her. Melanie was thinking about her cardboard door. She told her date that she had some schoolwork to finish, so she wouldn't be able to go to the movie. Her date was very disappointed. Melanie was terrified. She managed to get him to leave her apartment without kissing him.

She met a new possibility at a social gathering of other psychology graduate students. The new guy immediately complimented her. Compliments were Melanie's favorite candy. She gobbled them up.

Given her recent bad experiences, Melanie was careful to ask one of her peers about the new guy. Her friend gave Mr. Possibility a glowing recommendation. "From the moment you meet him, he makes you feel like you're his best friend," he said. Wow! That was promising. "But, he has a girlfriend back East," he warned. Oh. That wasn't so promising.

On their first date, Melanie questioned her potential "best friend" about the girlfriend. He reassured her that he had no prior commitments. They talked for hours. The man seemed to understand her like no one ever had. He knew instinctively that she wanted to be somebody. He told her over and over how she made him feel something he'd never felt before. He promised her he just wanted to be her friend.

The next day, Melanie felt like she had a hangover though she'd had nothing to drink. She felt sick and depressed. Like a hung-over drunk craving a morning drink, though, she longed for more of her new friend.

She learned that he had a complicated history. He hated his abusive father and had never loved his ex-wife. His therapist was helping him through all that and so was Melanie, he said. Melanie dreamed of being able to heal this broken man's heart, even as he was healing hers.

He called one day, excited to tell her that his girlfriend back East was buying his plane ticket so he could go see her. Once again, Melanie was shocked. "But you said she wasn't your girlfriend!" she cried. He explained that he meant he wasn't in a serious relationship with her. When Melanie asked if he intended to sleep with her during the visit, he said he did. Melanie was outraged. She told her "friend" exactly what she thought, but he flew off to have his fling.

Melanie had no plans to speak to him again. Then he called. He said how very much he'd missed her. How he'd thought of her the whole time he was gone. Hm. "Maybe he realized what a fool he's been," Melanie thought. She wasn't sure how it happened, but Melanie found herself back with her "friend."

When the girlfriend back East would call and talk to him in her presence, Melanie would have a temper tantrum, demanding that he end the relationship immediately. He would respond by telling Melanie that his therapist had said this was the only way he could do relationships "right now," because of his past. He further explained that his therapist thought Melanie had a lot of "issues."

Melanie was completely dumbfounded. Why on earth was she with this guy? Was there something really wrong with her? She felt like a drug addict who had no idea how she ended up on the street. But like that addict, she kept going back for more.

A defeated Melanie somehow found the strength to tell the man he had to make a choice. She went away for a few days with a girlfriend. She told him when she returned, he had to have an answer. The time away was like being in rehab. Melanie psyched herself up to hear that he had chosen the other woman. She told herself she would be okay. She deserved better. There were other men out there.

When she returned home, she was surprised and thrilled when her "friend" said, "I've decided I can't live without you." Melanie was high on love once again. What she didn't know was that her man meant he couldn't live without either woman. Until she discovered this, the man supplied Melanie with the fix she craved. She should have been happily ignorant, but she was miserable.

SHE WORKED HARD FOR THE MONEY

Melanie worked part-time in addition to her full-time graduate studies. She was hired as a research assistant for a psychologist at the hospital. Her boss was difficult to say the least. She instructed Melanie to begin researching a new topic. When Melanie reported her progress, she was told to stop working on the project immediately and she complied. At the next team meeting, however, she was asked why she didn't have the cancelled project completed.

In a private meeting, Melanie's supervisor asked her when the next team meeting was scheduled. Melanie said she didn't know, but would tell her when she could consult her notes in her office. Her boss yelled at her for not paying attention to important details. She then told Melanie to run a specific analysis on a data set that Melanie was not familiar with. When Melanie said she did not know how to do this analysis, she was berated for being ignorant.

Melanie decided that she did not want to continue working for this difficult woman the next year. But her boss reminded her constantly that if she didn't agree to work for her again, Melanie would be given a bad evaluation. A bad evaluation meant she might fail her graduate program. Failing the program meant she would have no chance of being accepted elsewhere. She didn't know what to do.

In addition to studying and working, Melanie counseled clients as a student therapist. Melanie had always been very busy, but the number of appointments and responsibilities she juggled had exceeded her ability to keep it all in her head. She was called one day by the counseling office and informed that she had missed a therapy appointment. Melanie was afraid she would be removed from the program for her error, so she faked an excuse.

Melanie's income and student loan allowed her to pay her rent and utilities and buy food and gas. There was nothing left over at the end of the month. When the brakes went out on her old car requiring a $600 repair, she was desperate. She put the entire bill on her credit card. She was only able to make the minimum payment and often she was late making that. Before long, she found herself using cash from one credit card to make the payment on the other.

She often didn't have money in her account for groceries or going out with friends. At those times, she wrote checks hoping they wouldn't bounce. They usually did. Paying the overdraft charges and late fees got her deeper and deeper into debt. Melanie dreamt of moving out of the dump she called home, but she had no idea how she would ever afford it.

DOWN AND OUT

At some point during her first year of graduate school, Melanie had a vague recognition that she was depressed. She knew without a doubt that she was anxious. She would sometimes hear a noise at night. She'd think about her cardboard door and she would freeze. Her fear paralyzed her and she would lie awake in her bed without moving for hours, certain that someone was going to harm her.

As Wonder Girl, Melanie had always had good grades. She never consulted anyone for help – not even her parents. Graduate school was extremely challenging for a girl who never asked for help.

She took an advanced statistics course that was required for her program. The professor's English was spoken with an accent, but everything he said sounded foreign to Melanie. After a while, she stopped taking notes. She didn't understand enough of what he was saying to write anything down. Soon, she quit even attempting to do her assignments. Fear and depression became her constant companions. She would lie on her bed trembling, allowing the roaches to join her uncontested.

MISERY LOVES COMPANY

Melanie had gone to church faithfully when she was attending a Christian college. She was hopeful about finding a new church home while she attended graduate school. She went to church a few times, held her breath, and introduced herself to some new people. Whenever she did, she seemed to be making people feel uncomfortable. The only people who acknowledged her presence were the youth group leaders. Melanie attended a few of their get-togethers, but she knew she didn't belong with high school students.

Melanie thought psychologists were supposed to be mentally healthy. That's why she never told anyone what she was going through. She was shocked by her fellow graduate students' tales of their past lives and experiences. They seemed just as shocked by Melanie's "sheltered life." Over time, Melanie found she had more and more in common with her new friends.

4

Whirling Around

A dead end street is a good place to turn around.
Naomi Judd

How did Melanie go from being stuck in a pit to being me, Wonder Woman? The same way Diana Prince did; she turned around. The Bible calls turning around "repentance." Repentance is what God, the Super Power, wants from us. "Repent! Turn away from all your offenses; then sin will not be your downfall" (Ezekiel 18:30b).

We can't understand what it means to turn, or repent, until we understand sin. That word 'sin' isn't a pleasant word to look at. For Melanie, 'sin' was like a bunch of roaches that lived in the dark. She didn't want to open the cupboard and see them in the light of day. But the longer she ignored the problem, the bigger it became.

At first, Melanie didn't know what a roach was and she didn't understand sin either. Was sin what landed one in prison? Was it the big stuff like murder and theft and fraud? Or was it little stuff like swearing and having sex with your boyfriend and not going to church?

Las Vegas, Nevada is known as "Sin City" to some today. In Biblical times, Sin was an Egyptian city, its name meaning "muddy," "a miry place," or "clayey."[7] Do you remember that we were made from clay? Our very nature is sin. Everything we do (or neglect to do) that is not what God wants is sin. What does God want? Perfection (Matthew 5:48).

That doesn't seem fair does it, expecting perfection? But think of it this way. Imagine that you have on a pure white wedding gown. It fairly glows it's so pristine. Now imagine that you see a bunch of kids who've been rolling in mud coming toward you. Are you going to let them anywhere near you? Of course not! Clean cannot abide with filth just as light cannot live with darkness (2 Corinthians 6:14). The only way you'd let those kids get close to you is if they were bathed and wearing clean clothes – new clothes would be preferable! If those kids weren't willing to take a bath – if they insisted they were clean enough – you wouldn't let them anywhere near you. In the same way, God will only allow us to be close if He cleans us. The first step in getting clean is repentance.

Repentance is recognizing that compared to a holy God, we are unclean. We are sin. We're made of it and we live in it and with it. We're selfish; we're foolish; we're arrogant; we're dishonest; we're lazy. Everything we do that isn't perfect is like another scoopful of mud thrown on us. But when we admit that we're dirty, and we're willing to be cleaned up, God will wash us and give us new clothes to wear. Then we can be close to Him again, just like the first Wonder Woman was in Paradise.

True repentance means we don't just change clothes, we ask God to change our minds and the direction of our lives. We turn around. Let me tell you about Melanie's turnaround.

CHECKING OUT

Melanie often spent the night with a neat and organized girlfriend who lived in a roach-free apartment. Melanie saw that life without bugs and people who bugged her was possible and preferable! She lived in a pit long enough to finally be motivated to get out.

She risked the wrath of her boss and worked more hours in a different department for someone else. She also applied for financial aid that would enable her to pay higher rent. She moved to a new apartment leaving the alcoholic, the batterer, and the stalker behind. She wanted to make sure she left the roaches behind, too. She checked every item obsessively to be sure no roaches tagged along. She slept like a baby in her clean home, though she didn't even have a bed at first. When she saw a couple of roaches in the first weeks, she had nightmares about them. The roaches weren't the only ones who stowed away and gave her nightmares.

Melanie was ecstatic when her boyfriend told her he'd ended his relationship with his East coast girlfriend for good. Then she was furious when he told her he was excited about a date he had planned with a new woman. He couldn't understand why Melanie was angry and Melanie couldn't understand why it was killing her not to call him. It didn't help when he left everything she'd given him (plus some things she hadn't) on her front porch. He was obviously trying to suck her back into the relationship. Somehow she found the strength to evict that roach from her life.

CHECKING IN

Melanie told her statistics professor the truth about why she hadn't been doing her assignments. She got caught up and asked for help when she needed it. She also started using a planner to make sure she didn't miss appointments.

School, work, finances and relationships continued to be a struggle for Melanie, but things slowly started turning around. She began exercising regularly and started exercising better judgment with men.

When she met Clark Kent and began discussing marriage, Superman and I took charge. We discussed our old selves' failures in past relationships and admitted we needed the Super Power. We joined a church and gave God control of our marriage. I felt I had been reborn.

I fearfully admitted to my fiancé how indebted I was with credit card debt, student loans, and car payments. I was overwhelmed with gratitude when he did not reject me. Instead, he paid off all my debts and even bought me new clothes to wear.

When we met with the pastor of the church we chose to be married in, I was afraid I would have to explain Melanie's behavior. I didn't. I wore a beautiful white wedding gown and became a member of two new families: my husband's and the church. The church listed my name as Melanie Wilson, but they seemed to understand I was really Wonder Woman.

TURNING AROUND

Are you ready to turn your back on your old life and begin life anew? I cannot promise you that you will marry a man who will pay off your debts, but I can promise you something better. If you are willing to walk away from the ashes of your old life and wear a new clean gown like Cinderella did, the Prince will come and pay off what you owe. You no longer have to be a slave to the filth and the sin in your life. The Prince has purchased your freedom. He isn't shocked by the dirt in your life, nor will He reject you. Cinderella didn't hang her head at the ball. She knew she was clean. Would you like to be sure you're clean? Would you like to live like the princess you were created to be?

WHERE ARE YOU GOING?

We all know Wonder Woman flies an invisible jet, but real Wonder Women start off driving. We never turn around until we admit we're going the wrong way. If we persist in believing there's nothing wrong with the way we're living, we're going to be lost.

Melanie thought she was on the right road. She comforted herself with the idea that bright, creative people are necessarily slobs. She told herself that premarital sex was fine as long as you loved someone. She compared herself to alcoholics and figured her problems were only "bad habits."

She was driving along fine until the brakes went out on her car. Melanie didn't know where the road was leading and she didn't have the self-control she needed to stop herself when she got off track. She could have used the Bible as her road map and called upon God as her OnStar, but she didn't.

What's your final destination? What do you want life to look like a year from now? Or five or ten or twenty? What do you want your life after death to be like? Are you on the highway to heaven? Or the road to – well, you know.

In your desire for a changed life, you may have considered the saying, "The road to hell is paved with good intentions." That's absolutely true. That's a good saying to reflect upon when you want to be weighed down with guilt. It's also true that the highway to Heaven is paved with Jesus' good deeds. He is the way to heaven. He paid all of our tolls and obeyed every "traffic" law. We're good to go! That, my Wonder Sister, is the Good News.

The highway to heaven is free: free of guilt and free of payment of any kind (Ephesians 2:8-9). We want to follow Jesus on that highway, living the way He lived, but our ticket to Heaven is pre-paid. When we try to pay for it with our church attendance, charitable giving, and good deeds, it's as if we're saying the price He paid wasn't high enough.

That ticket cost Jesus everything. The payment for sin is death. You can't call a ticket fixer for sin. Only death will do. Jesus paid our debt by dying on a cross, not for His sins, but for ours. Jesus was without sin (2 Corinthians 5:21). He was the perfectly clean Son who made it possible for us to be clean and close to God.

If you're not following Jesus on the highway to Heaven, may I suggest you turn around? Admit you are going the wrong way and that you don't have the power to stop the car. Carrie Underwood's song, "Jesus Take the Wheel," is about an old self who turns around:

Jesus take the wheel;
Take it from my hands;
I can't do this on my own.
I'm letting go,
So give me one more chance.
Save me from this road I'm on.
Jesus take the wheel.

A true Wonder Woman always drives to her destination sitting in the passenger seat. Move over and let Jesus drive.

When your Super Power pays your debt and starts driving, you will be overwhelmed with gratitude. It's like the Prince telling Cinderella she doesn't have to run away at midnight. It's like living a real-life Fairy Tale.

GET BACK ON TRACK

Some of you are like Melanie. You were on the right road, but somehow you got off track. You were on the highway to Heaven, Jesus had the wheel, and then you started inching your way back into the driver's seat. Truth be told, you thought you might be able to take a shortcut. Jesus' way seemed really long. And who likes to read maps? You figured if you headed north, you'd get there. But the longer you drove, the more confused you became. Was there really a true north? Or does everyone decide what's north for them? Your old self is a terrible back seat driver, so you let her drive for a while just to keep her quiet. You're not sure how long you were sleeping, but you know for sure that your life started heading south.

The first step in getting your life back on track is to strap your old self in a car seat (got any duct tape?). Second, get back in the passenger seat. And third, study the landmarks so you'll know you're on the right road. The Bible describes these landmarks as fruit. The brat in the back will be screaming that she doesn't want fruit. She wants fast food and she wants to drive! If the brat agrees that change is good, she wants it so everyone will be amazed by her. She wants a changed life because she wants fun and excitement. She wants a changed life because she thinks it will be easier. If she can't be the life of the party, she prefers to park the car.

Have you heard Jeff Foxworthy's list of "You might be a redneck if…"? My Wonder Sister, your brat might be driving the car if:

You want to lose weight so everyone will compliment you and will think you're attractive.

You want to be more organized so your friends and co-workers will look up to you.

You want your kids to behave better to impress people.

You want to get out of debt so you can have the clothes, the house, and the car you deserve.

The first Wonder Woman wanted to eat some fruit to be wise. We Wonder Women want to produce fruit we can share with others. The Bible's book of Galatians tells us that when Wonder Woman has Jesus driving the car and her old self in the back seat, we can expect to see the fruit of love, joy, peace, patience, kindness, goodness, faithfulness, gentleness and self-control in our lives.

A fruit tree doesn't produce fruit to make itself look good. Instead, the fruit produced makes the grower look good and the people who eat it feel good. If a fruit tree had feelings, it would enjoy producing fruit because that is what it was created to do. We Wonder Women do have feelings and we enjoy the fruit we see God growing in our lives. If we're off the beaten path and we don't see fruit for a while, we need to let go of the wheel and let Jesus take us back to the highway.

FUEL UP

The cartoon character Fred Flintsone provided the power for his car with his own legs and he never got far. In fact, he always ended up in trouble. If we Wonder Women want to lead changed lives, we have to remember where our power comes from. Ephesians 6:10 tells us, "Finally, be strong in the Lord and in his mighty power." We wouldn't dream of trying to drive a car without gas in the tank, but when it comes to turning our lives around, we so often try to get by on our own strength. It's no wonder we complain about running on fumes.

The Bible says that believing in our own strength is like worshiping ourselves (Habakkuk 1:11). We talk about our willpower or lack thereof all the time as though change depends on a trait we either have or don't have. Yet God says that He is the one who gives us willpower (Philippians 2:13). He's the gas that runs the car and He's even willing to drive! We get where He wants us to go much faster if we stop trying to push the car down the road and just enjoy the ride.

Why on earth would we use our own strength when we can call on the Super Power's mighty right arm? We aren't content being Wonder Women. Remember the first Wonder Woman's mistake once again. She had it all, but she wanted more. She wondered what it would be like to be God and she thought the fruit might get her there.

My mother enjoys talking about Melanie at two. She told Melanie to do something and Melanie replied, "If you think you're woman enough to make me!" My mother tells me she was more than woman enough! The two-year-old you have in the back of your car wants to drive and she doesn't think you're woman enough to make her sit still. She wants to be her own mother, even her own god. In the movie, *The Incredibles*, Buddy was like that arrogant two-year-old who thought his own smarts were enough to make him a superhero. Really, he was no more than a brat playing dress up, wreaking havoc. Eventually, he got a whoopin', reminding us that no matter how intelligent we are and no matter how much technology we have available to us, we can't be superheroes without the Super Power.

No one fills up their gas tank unless they think they need fuel. Will you admit you're running on empty? Will you admit that pushing the car is getting awfully tiring?

There is no program for addictions more successful than the 12-step program. The program's first step is to admit you are powerless to change. You may or may not have an addiction, but the first step toward lasting change is the same. Can you relate to the alcoholic quoted on the 12-step website?

> Step 1 is the first step to freedom. I admit to myself that something is seriously wrong in my life. I have created messes in my life. Perhaps my whole life is a mess, or maybe just important parts are a mess. I admit this and quit trying to play games with myself anymore. I realize that my life has become unmanageable in many ways. It is not under my control anymore. I do things that I later regret doing and tell myself that I will not do them again. But I do. I keep on doing them, in spite of my regrets, my denials, my vows, my cover-ups and my facades.[8]

You probably are very much aware of the mess you've made of your life. I know I was. I am not asking you to wallow in guilt and shame. On the contrary, admitting you are powerless to change is the first step toward a free ride.

Even those of us who truly desire change have a hard time with this step. We tend to think, "I'm not powerless! If my kids would help...If my husband didn't get in the way...If I worked fewer hours...If I just found the right system..."

In the midst of a recent power outage in our home, my 4-year-old son asked, "Mom, which TV works?" Like my son, we have a hard time wrapping our brains around the idea that we don't have power. We think we just haven't flipped the right switch or pressed the right button. No matter how many times you read your car's manual, no matter how many buttons you push, no matter how much you want the car to move, it's not going anywhere without gas. Turn the car around, get into the passenger seat, and get some gas.

You may not know how to refuel from a spiritual perspective. Don't worry. Chapter 8, the "Weapons of Change" will tell you how. Turning around seems simple enough. Why then is lasting change so difficult? We'll address that question next.

Why it's So Hard to Change

Change is the end result of all true learning.
Leo Buscaglia

O*Magazine* recently ran an article that claimed to answer the question, "Why is it so difficult to change?" The article seemed to offer new information with its impressive descriptions of brain scan research. But the material isn't new. Melanie had learned it years before she found herself in a pit.

KNOWLEDGE

Melanie was certain that with enough knowledge, she could solve her own problems and everyone else's, too. In college, her psychology professor used rats to demonstrate how problem behaviors developed and how they could be fixed. The answer was really so simple! Whatever was rewarded would be repeated. Whatever was not rewarded (or punished) would be eradicated. Eureka!

Melanie watched her professor put these behavioral principles into practice in his own classroom. He rewarded students for good grades by praising them in front of the class. Nothing was more effective in motivating Melanie than praise, so she delighted in studying for this particular class.

The lab portion of the class required Melanie and her lab partner to train rats to do a variety of behaviors: press a bar, look through a window, swing on a trapeze and play "basketball" with a marble. Melanie was sure she had the knowledge she needed to finish her lab assignment with all the studying she'd done.

The rats weren't fully fed so they would be hungry and motivated. At first, whenever the rat came close to the red bar in his cage, he would be rewarded with a food pellet. After a while, Melanie and her lab partner waited until the rat moved closer and closer to the bar before giving him a pellet. Finally, he was required to depress the bar completely to get a pellet. Melanie was elated at how quickly they had been able to train a rat to bar press, and all without language!

Learning the behavior came easily for the rat; unlearning it came hard. At first the rat was given a food pellet every time he pressed the bar. Later the young women changed the rules. Sometimes they gave him a food pellet after two presses, sometimes after five presses, and other times after ten or more. Eventually, the lab instructions required the behavior to be extinguished completely. Melanie and her partner had to sit for what seemed like hours until the rat had not pressed the bar at all to prove that the behavior had truly been eliminated.

Near the end of a very long period of no bar pressing, when the girls would have been able to record a successful extinction, Melanie's lab partner accidentally hit the pellet button. The rat resumed pressing the bar like a video-game-addicted kid. Rats!

The young psychology student had learned that rewards and consequences had an impact on learning, but there was more to it. There was an unknown variability that had to be taken into account. Sometimes learning and unlearning didn't happen according to plan.

Melanie's professor encouraged his students to apply principles of learning and behavior to correct their own problems. Melanie was in heaven! Not only would she fix the problem with overeating that had plagued her for so long, but she would be praised in class for doing so!

Melanie joined a campus weight loss group and learned about calorie and fat content of foods and calorie expenditure (exercise). She memorized her calorie counter and her friends frequently relied on her expertise. "How many calories in a cinnamon roll?" Usually the answer depressed, but didn't dissuade the asker. Despite her role as the Calorie Queen, Melanie's weight didn't come off. She was certain that adding behavioral principles to her plan was the key. She would simply reward herself for eating well and exercising.

Melanie was already being rewarded for getting up early in the morning to swim or run. She felt great! She also found it rewarding to eat less and avoid the stuffed-to-the-gills sensation. Unfortunately, sleeping in and eating to excess were rewarding, too. Melanie hadn't counted on that. The rat had no other means of reward in his controlled environment other than pleasing the experimenter for a pellet. Melanie's environment wasn't so controlled. She had roommates who convinced her that ordering pizza would be fun. And nothing she had learned in the lab had taught her how to say no to that.

Melanie figured she was missing some vital information that would help her change. She hung out in the self-help section of the bookstore and found two books that talked about the dangers of dieting. Both books argued that dieting caused weight problems. That certainly made sense to Melanie. She had never had a real concern with her weight until she started yo-yo dieting in high school. She learned that eating for reasons other than physical hunger and failing to stop when she was satisfied (not full) was the source of her problem. She determined to quit dieting for good.

Melanie lost weight and told everyone she knew how she'd done it. She quit worrying about calorie content and began eating exactly what she wanted as long as she was truly hungry. Melanie felt she had proved the theory that with enough knowledge, people could solve their own problems. Knowledge can be defined as "acquaintance with facts, truths, or principles, as from study or investigation."[5] Melanie no longer stuffed herself with food, but she was full to overflowing with knowledge.

UNDERSTANDING

Although Melanie never regained to her highest weight, her weight loss didn't last. She had learned how to lose weight and keep it off by eating according to hunger and fullness, but she was unable to maintain this natural approach to eating.

She also knew she was eating to cope with her emotions. She ate when she was happy to celebrate. She ate because she was stressed. She ate when she was sad. She ate when she was bored. She understood what drove the eating, but she didn't understand why she couldn't master it.

In her late 20s, Melanie's weight didn't appear to be a problem. But food and her inability to control her eating habits weighed heavily on Melanie's mind. Her weight fluctuated by ten pounds, sometimes within one week, because of out-of-control eating. Food was her first thought in the morning and her weight was her last thought at night.

One day at the grocery store checkout lane, she saw an article title on the front page of *Woman's Day* magazine asking, "Can God Make You Thin?" Melanie bought the magazine and read the article with great anticipation. It was about a Christian weight loss program. At the time, Melanie was involved in a church and wanted to know God better. The program sounded great! The testimonials motivated her to order the materials. She asked permission to make the class available to others at her church and was granted it. She knew the power of social support.

In the course of the workshop, Melanie learned that her overeating could be called idol worship. One of the Ten Commandments in the Bible prohibited God's people from worshiping objects as gods. Because Melanie had never prayed to a statue, she couldn't imagine that she had ever worshiped an idol, but she began to see food as a false god. When she had a problem or just wanted to celebrate, she ran to Taco Bell. She learned that God wanted to be her one and only God. He didn't want to be runner-up to a plate of nachos.

Melanie felt she finally had understanding – "to be thoroughly familiar with; apprehend clearly the character, nature, or subtleties of."[5] She was truly sorry for her idol worship and prayed daily for help. At first, she experienced great success. Melanie was so pleased because she was able to teach other class members at church how to have the same success.

After several weeks of consistent weight loss, however, Melanie was no longer able to control herself. No matter how determined she was to eat in a way that pleased God, she couldn't do it. She would find herself eating past full again and eating out of emotion. She was so frustrated because she had seen the testimonies of others who had been successful in losing weight this way. Why not her? Here she was encouraging others in the class when she was failing.

One day when she had once again succumbed to the urge to overeat, Melanie cried out to God, "I can't do it! I give up! If you want me to stop overeating, YOU do it! I quit!" Weeks later I realized this moment was the end of Melanie's weight fluctuations and obsession with food. This freedom with food and weight management continued much to her astonishment.

WISDOM

When people ask me as Wonder Woman how I am able to stay so slim, I cannot tell them how it happened except to say that God did it. I now have something more valuable than knowledge and understanding. I have wisdom – "knowledge of what is true or right coupled with just judgment as to action."[5] I know Melanie was wrong to look to the false god of food for my comfort and help. I know Melanie was missing out on blessings because of her overeating. And I learned she was powerless to solve her own problem. Only when I admitted that and allowed my Super Power to change the Melanie in me did I find victory. The victory over obsession with food and weight was won for me over ten years ago.

READINESS FOR CHANGE

Melanie's doctoral research was on the Stages of Change.[6] She studied people's readiness to change and its effect on actual change. She learned that some individuals are not ready to change, no matter how much they say they are. These are the people who really like to eat, smoke, or drink, for example, and aren't willing to give up the rewards of their habits.

There are also people who are seriously thinking about change. These are the individuals whose doctors and spouses have told them they must change. These are people who know they would be so much happier "if only." They start checking into treatment options or visiting gyms.

A third group consists of individuals who are actively making change. They are eating differently, going to AA, or seeing a therapist, for example.

Finally, there are those who have made significant changes and are working at maintaining those changes.

Proverbs, a book of wisdom in the Bible, may be speaking of these different groups of people when it compares knowledge, understanding, and wisdom to building a house:

By wisdom a house is built, and through understanding it is established; through knowledge its rooms are filled with rare and beautiful treasures (24:3-4).

Those, like Melanie, who first collect knowledge are like those who aren't ready to change. They have some interesting facts about change, but that's all. Those who have knowledge and understanding only are like those who are thinking about change. They know why they should change and they'd like to change, but they haven't begun building the foundation of change. Those with wisdom are like those who live in a sturdy home and are maintaining it.

Trying to change without wisdom is like being a homeless woman who carries all her treasures of knowledge with her everywhere she goes. Trying to solve problems with understanding alone is like a homeless woman trying to set up housekeeping on a park bench. Wisdom gives us a home for all the understanding and knowledge we have gained.

If you're living like a homeless woman, my Wonder Sister, let me hand you the keys to your new house. Proverbs 2:6 says, "For the LORD gives wisdom, and from his mouth come knowledge and understanding." The Super Power, the God who created you, the Lord of the universe is the source of wisdom, knowledge and understanding. If we lack wisdom, we have only to ask Him for it (James 1:5).

Yet some of us are not ready to do that. We prefer to keep reading *O Magazine*, going to seminars, and talking about change, rather than really experiencing it. Some recent research suggests that even talking about our plans to change makes us feel better. Melanie was like that. Like Gary Heavin, she had to reach the end of herself before she was willing to ask God for help.

Gary opened a chain of fitness centers in Texas. He was interested in fitness and had the knowledge he needed to run the business. Before long, however, the high overhead required to run amenity-heavy fitness centers led to financial problems and eventually to bankruptcy. His wife left him, he lost custody of his two children, and he was arrested for failure to pay child support. During his six months in jail, Gary read the Bible and recommitted his life to Jesus.

With newfound wisdom and purpose, Gary and his new wife opened a simple fitness center for women. The concept of a 30-minute, no-frills workout was a success. Today, with 7,000 workout centers, Curves is the largest fitness franchise in the world. God's wisdom won't make us all millionaires, but it can help us rebuild our lives.

You may be hoping I will give you the latest psychological techniques or information about pills or treatments that can change your life, but that's just knowledge. If knowledge had the power to change us, Melanie would be a testimony to that. She's not. Wisdom from God is what we need to live as Wonder Women. When we have wisdom, the knowledge about how to eat, how to exercise, and how to stay sober becomes useful.

Are you ready for some real wisdom? If so, get ready for a fight. Wonder Woman has numerous enemies who want to make sure she doesn't succeed in the battle for change.

6

Who We're Fighting

Reaching back to Ancient Egypt, there's been a single cabal of powerful
individuals directing the course of human history. But the common man
prefers to believe they don't exist, which aids their success.

"The Justice League"

Unfortunately, our troubles don't end when we whirl around and choose a new path. Instead, we often find the opposition to change grows. Standing between us and our goals are some formidable enemies.

Some of us assume we have no enemies. Others of us think our children, husbands, bosses, friends, and doctors are the foes behind the masks. Sometimes we are right in assuming that even those closest to us are not fighting for us. But the Bible tells us we are at war with another enemy – the true source of all our opposition. He is the same enemy we Wonder Women have had since the beginning:

> Put on the full armor of God so that you can take your stand against the devil's schemes. For our struggle is not against flesh and blood, but against the rulers, against the authorities, against the powers of this dark world and against the spiritual forces of evil in the heavenly realms (Ephesians 6:11-12).

We'll talk about our armor in the next chapter. For now, know that the devil is our ultimate nemesis. He has in mind nothing but evil for us. He does not want you and me to be Wonder Women because he hates the Super Power. He covets our love for God and does whatever he can to cause us to doubt Him.

JOB, A SUPERMAN

The Bible's book of Job (pronounced like Joe with a b) tells of one of the greatest clashes between a superhero and the enemy, Satan. Job was a Superman who loved the Super Power and had been blessed as a result. He had many children and great wealth. When the Super Power spoke with Satan about Job, Satan suggested the only reason Job served God was because he had so much. God gave Satan permission to take the blessings away from Job as a test.

In no time, Job lost all of his children, his possessions, his health, and the respect of friends. When Job didn't hear from the Super Power for a long time, he assumed God was his enemy. That was exactly what Satan had in mind. Job didn't know Satan was permitted to attack him to test his faith in God.

When the cancer, the betrayal, or the job loss comes, we have to know God permits hardship for our good (Romans 8:28). God wants us to turn to Him for strength, wisdom, and faith in the midst of these battles. Satan wants us to turn to him instead, becoming like him – angry, selfish, and believing we are god enough to change ourselves. When we turn to Satan, we become part of his army – unwittingly becoming someone else's opponent.

There are many enemies in the devil's army. The comic book Wonder Woman has fought several of them. I will describe the most powerful adversaries to the process of change and will tell you how we may defeat them with the Super Power.

PERFECTION

Perfection is an enemy who attacks Wonder Girl in an effort to obtain the secrets of the Amazons. She suggests change isn't worthwhile unless it is perfect change. By pursuing perfection, she hopes to find the secret to being the Super Power.

Perfection attacked me as Wonder Girl. When I was sent to clean my room, Perfection came and said that picking up the room wasn't enough. To be truly powerful, I must clean out my closet and my dresser drawers, too. I believed what Perfection had to say, so at the end of a long day of cleaning, I had piles of belongings all over the floor. I didn't have time to sort perfectly, so at dinner time I threw it all back in the closet and drawers. When I was discouraged by my still-messy room, Perfection said, "Better to do it right or not at all."

Perfection attacked me again when I was trying to lose weight. When I ate something that wasn't on the diet or didn't exercise as planned, she said, "Better to start again next week when you can have a perfect record. You may as well enjoy your food and leisure now." I took her advice many times.

Perfection attacked me again when I was in graduate school. When I struggled in my coursework and in organizing my research, she said, "Everyone else in your class is doing perfectly well. Don't tell anyone you need help until you have it all figured out." I took her advice many times.

Perfection attacked me again when I became a mother. When I struggled with impatience and discipline, she said, "All the other mothers know how to correct behavior problems calmly. Don't tell anyone you don't have control until you know how to manage your child yourself." I took her advice many times.

Perfection attacked me again when I wanted to write a book. When I started writing, she said, "You need an agent, a publisher, a full-time speaking career, and until your life is perfectly changed, you don't have anything to say." I believed her for many years.

Even when things really are perfect, Perfection will come. I know because she came to the first Wonder Woman. The first Wonder Woman had a beautiful home, plenty to eat, a loving husband, and a close relationship with the Super Power. She was never hurt, frightened, or sick. But Perfection suggested Wonder Woman could have more – should have more. And Wonder Woman believed her (Genesis 3).

After what happened (which we refer to as the Fall), our lives are no longer perfect. Our homes may be messy, falling apart, or too expensive. Our food may be scarce, contributing to obesity, or making us sick. Our husbands may be indifferent, controlling, or dependent. But we still have something perfect: the Super Power. He hasn't changed and He never will. He is still able to meet every one of our needs *perfectly*.

How can we prevail over Perfection? First, by pressing on. Paul says, "Not that I have already obtained all this, or have already been made perfect, but I press on to take hold of that for which Christ Jesus took hold of me" (Philippians 3:12). Can you imagine a runner in mid-race who imagines his start was imperfect and quits? Ridiculous! Yet, this is what we so often do. Rather than focus on the goal ahead, we look behind us, bemoaning what could have been.

One of my preschoolers was constantly running into things like side-view mirrors in a parking lot because of his habit of looking behind him when he walked. When we focus on our imperfect past, we get hurt. Then we say things to ourselves we wouldn't allow anyone else to say: "You're pitiful. A loser. Why do you even bother trying? Quit before you make a complete fool of yourself." We wonder why we've failed.

When I was first learning to FLY (see Chapter 9), I looked behind me a lot. I saw a lot of things I hadn't done perfectly and I was tempted to give up. Instead, I focused on how far I had come. So there were a few times I hadn't shined my sink and made my bed! Before learning to FLY, I did them rarely if at all. I also kept my eyes on the finish line. I learned the only definition of failure: dropping out of the race. Change will come if we do as Paul, an imperfect man, did: "I have fought the good fight, I have finished the race, I have kept the faith" (2 Timothy 4:7). Keep plodding along like the tortoise who beat the hare.

The second way to overcome Perfection is to boast about our weaknesses. Many times I have asked God to just change me – in an instant, please! But His plan for change is often more like a four-course dinner than a drive-through meal. Paul knew the feeling. He said, "To keep me from becoming conceited because of these surpassingly great revelations, there was given me a thorn in my flesh, a messenger of Satan, to torment me. Three times I pleaded with the Lord to take it away from me" (2 Corinthians 12:7-8).

Perhaps you know Perfection or another opponent is attacking you and you wonder why the Lord is not fighting for you. Paul continues:

But he said to me, 'My grace is sufficient for you, for my power is made perfect in weakness.' Therefore I will boast all the more gladly about my weaknesses, so that Christ's power may rest on me. That is why, for Christ's sake, I delight in weaknesses, in insults, in hardships, in persecutions, in difficulties. For when I am weak, then I am strong (2 Corinthians 12:7-10).

This word makes it clear we will never change if we insist on perfectly following the Weight Watchers rules or going every day without smoking, for example. The Super Power works in us when we admit how weak we are.

One of the things I so admire about friends who are long-time AA members is their constant affirmation of their powerlessness over alcohol. They boast in this weakness and make it possible for the Super Power to do His perfect work. Boasting in our weakness is merely stating the truth that we are not God. This truth sets us free (John 8:32).

When Perfection comes (and you know she will), agree with her:

Yes, I'm incapable of maintaining an orderly home.
Yes, I'm incapable of saving money.
Yes, I'm incapable of exercising regularly.

Then say, "But thanks be to the Super Power who is more than capable! Hallelujah!" The way to defeat Perfection is not by striving for perfection, but by admitting we can do nothing without God (John 15:5).

The third way to defeat Perfection is by aiming for the Honor Roll. A boy in my high school math class constantly argued with the teacher when one of his answers was marked wrong. It drove him crazy not to have a perfect paper, though he was earning a high A in the class. He's a doctor now and I wonder what difference those few red marks have made in his life. What do you think?

We make it possible for Perfection to defeat us when we adopt one of her goals:

> I'm going to walk every day this month, no matter what the weather.
> I will lose two pounds a week until summer.
> I will not yell at my kids again *ever*.

These goals are as silly as a student striving for 100% in each and every class. We set ourselves up for failure and then we quit – exactly what Perfection has in mind.

My friend Marla Cilley, the FLYLady, has a saying: "Housework done incorrectly still blesses your family." If you don't dust the ceiling fans every week, but you do feather dust your furniture regularly, your work is still meaningful. If you walk most days, you're going to be fitter and probably trimmer. If you are eating less most days, you're going to be healthier and leaner. If you're speaking calmly to your children most of the time, you'll all be happier for it.

But Perfection says anything less than 100% isn't worth doing. Does a 100% standard motivate you? It doesn't me. I never feel like I'm "there." As good a student as I was, I never achieved 100% in every class. But I was an honor student.

Schools usually have an A and a B honor roll. Honor students' work is correct 80% to 90% of the time. And that's on average. Some honor roll students make up for a poor score on one test with an excellent one on another.

Are students achieving less than 100% denied college or jobs? Of course not! Yet, we've believed Perfection when she says 80% to 90% success isn't worthy of reward. If we change most habits 80% to 90% of the time, we will achieve the changes we want. Of course there are exceptions. A wife who is faithful 80% to 90% of the time isn't worthy of praise. Drug and alcohol use may be another exception. Aim for the Honor Roll and when you achieve it, celebrate it! Something that supports you in changing would be great (e.g., a new outfit for losing weight, a new pair of shoes for exercising, a charitable donation for curbing spending).

DUKE OF DECEPTION

Another of the comic-book Wonder Woman's antagonists is the Duke of Deception, a war monger. The Duke attempts to trick us into using his weapons – weapons that can destroy us.

The Duke's favorite weapon is anger. He says if we just get good and angry, we can whip this thing. He says our abusive mom, our neglectful dad, our incompetent boss, our betraying friend, our lazy husband, our ungrateful kids, and that slow driver in front of us all deserve what's coming to them. If it weren't for them, says the Duke, we could change or we would have been okay in the first place. The deception is that anger is just an emotion. All we must do, says the Duke, is express it and we will be healed.

I believed the Duke and recommended that my clients express their anger by ripping telephone books and screaming at an empty chair representing their guilty party.

Although clients often reported feeling better initially, I noticed that they continued to carry anger and resentment for past injustices. Hot anger became a cold war and there was no change.

Believing the Duke's lie led me to write to Teri Maxwell, author of *Managers of Their Homes*. In her online newsletter, she wrote of her remorse for being angry with her children when they didn't pick up their belongings as directed. She hadn't yelled at her children, so I didn't see the problem. In fact, I worried about her suppressed anger becoming depression. I wrote on and on as if I were the Duke of Deception. I said anger was just an emotion, neither good nor bad, and expressing it wasn't wrong.

Mrs. Maxwell wrote me back, explaining that an audiotape by Dr. S.M. Davis had changed her perspective on anger. She said if I would agree to listen to the tape, she would send it to me at no charge.

I figured I had nothing to lose, so agreed to listen. When I received the tape, I put it aside to listen to later. When I looked for it, it was missing. I was, of course, angry! I couldn't find it for several weeks and had decided to just pay for another tape. I was embarrassed that I wasn't able to respond to Mrs. Maxwell's generosity with an opinion.

One morning as I was preparing to leave for an appointment in the city, I saw the tape lying in the middle of the kitchen floor. I couldn't believe the timing of finding the tape, given that I had a good period of time to listen to it as I drove. I was amazed at what I heard. The Bible, said Dr. Davis, did not recommend that we freely express anger. On the contrary, it said, "Refrain from anger and turn from wrath; do not fret—it leads only to evil" (Psalm 37:8). Anger was also likened to sexual immorality, witchcraft, and drunkenness (Galatians 5:19-21).

Dr. Davis spoke about how destructive anger had been in the life of Moses, the man who led the Israelites out of Egypt. If you're not familiar with the Bible, you may know him as the man Charlton Heston portrayed in *The Ten Commandments*. Moses had to run for his life after his anger at an Egyptian soldier led to the soldier's death (Exodus 2). His anger at the rebellious Israelites led him to smash the tablets on which God had written the Ten Commandments (Exodus 32:19). And his anger led to his disobedience when bringing water from a rock, and eventually his death before entering the Promised Land (Numbers 20:9-12).

Dr. Davis's point was that God is capable of justly handling the weapon of anger and we are not. In fact, most of the Bible's verses having to do with anger refer to God's anger. When we are angry, it is often because we are trying to be God. We judge and want to take revenge though God specifically forbids it (Romans 12:19).

Finally, Dr. Davis pointed out that it wasn't just yelling and fighting that were wrong, but even the spirit of anger. I knew what he was talking about. I knew people whose words couldn't be faulted, but in whom I sensed resentment and bitterness. He also explained that anger didn't have to be constant to be destructive. He asked one occasionally angry man if he would like to live next to a volcano that only erupted every so often.

Anger, claimed Dr. Davis, was the number one reason a child rebelled. He cited examples of families in which parents dealt with their anger problem and found their rebellious teens were restored to the family. I was impressed. I listened to the rest of the tape on the way home from my appointment and became determined not to bring the weapon of anger into my home again. I committed to not becoming angry or even having a spirit of anger.

I came home to a gallon of spilled milk, a messy house, fighting kids, and an irritable husband. I didn't get angry; I cried. Over the course of that very trying day, I realized that I was angry constantly. I had always thought my husband had the problem with anger – not me. Over the next few months of attempting to lay that weapon down, I learned my anger fanned my husband's into a raging fire. It also fueled the fights between my children and occasionally caused rebellion, too.

Not long after listening to Dr. Davis, I was asked to do a call-in radio show. The caller was having trouble with her son refusing to go to bed. His behavior at school was fine, but at home, he was obstinate. I honestly didn't know what the answer was for her, but asked, "Can I ask if you or your husband has a problem with anger?" I was surprised when she humbly answered, "Yes, I do." We discussed how she might overcome her anger and she seemed pleased with the solution I offered.

The Duke of Deception wants us to believe that our anger is an effective impetus for change for others and for us, too. Yet, even self-directed anger leads to rebellion. We usually do exactly what angers us about ourselves. We eat more ice cream, spend more money, and surf the web all day. Anger at other people who have hurt us rarely results in change either. Usually, the offender doesn't know we're angry, doesn't care, or gets angry in return. On the contrary, forgiveness often brings change. It may not restore the relationship, but it can restore us.

Janice McBride's life story is one of unthinkable abuse perpetrated by and permitted by her mother. Janice's mother tried to abort her more than once and frequently told her she wished Janice had never been born. She was physically, sexually, and emotionally abused. As an adult, Janice received the Super Power through faith in Jesus. She felt led to visit her mother and care for her, though her mother lived thousands of miles away in Scotland. Janice's mother asked Janice how she could forgive her when she had been so terrible to her. Janice said, "The question is, how could Jesus forgive me?" Janice's mother also received the Super Power by faith in Jesus because of Janice's love and forgiveness.[9]

To lay down the weapon of anger:

Contemplate what you've been forgiven. Our anger, like Moses', isn't justified because we are imperfect sinners – no better than those who hurt or disappoint us.

Commit to letting go of anger. Ask people to keep you accountable. Understand that laying down the weapon of anger may be a higher priority for God than the other goals you have.

Concentrate on the destructiveness of anger and the blessings of letting it go. Order Dr. Davis's tape,

"Freedom from the Spirit of Anger," at his website, www.solvefamilyproblems.com.

Check your thoughts. A simple reassessment of the situation can eliminate anger. "I'm such an idiot!" becomes "I made a mistake anyone could make." "The kids never pick up their toys!" becomes "They were so happy playing together, they got distracted."

Wonder Women have powerful weapons, but no matter what the Duke of Deception says, we don't use the weapon of anger in the battle for change.

DOCTOR PSYCHO

One of the most dangerous of the comic book Wonder Woman's enemies, Dr. Psycho went insane after another man took his woman. Demented Dr. Psycho's weapons are telepathic, psychic, and spiritual powers.

Melanie tried Dr. Psycho's weapons in high school. She read a book about ESP and did what the book suggested in order to read others' thoughts. She wasn't upset because she failed; she was terrified because she succeeded. In college, she met a young man who'd had a similar experience. He found when he played cards, he knew what the other players were holding. When he told his father about this unnatural ability, his father said, "That kind of power can only come from God or Satan and I don't think God is concerned with you winning card games." My friend laid down the weapon and was no longer able to "read" others' cards.

Melanie also saw a psychic "for fun" in college. She hoped she could find out if she would marry her long-term boyfriend. Somehow she thought affirmation from the psychic would make her boyfriend's avoidant, rejecting behavior more acceptable. The psychic agreed Melanie would marry the boyfriend and would have four children, some of them adopted (she didn't).

Melanie also read horoscopes and New Age books for entertainment. She figured there was no harm in believing the newspaper could predict her future and a book could help her think herself rich. She was especially tempted by the easy solutions Dr. Psycho offered to her problems.

But Wonder Women don't use these weapons because they put us in danger. Laurette Willis, founder of PraiseMoves, says she not only practiced yoga exercises, but became entranced by the religion of yoga. Now a Wonder Woman, Laurette calls yoga "the missionary arm of Hinduism and the New Age movement."[10] How does the worshiping of powers other than the Super Power God put us in danger? Worshiping other gods, consulting psychics, and trusting in predictions like horoscopes are all condemned by God and provoke Him to anger (e.g., 2 Kings 21:6). The first commandment is to love and worship God as your one and only God (Exodus 20:3). Satan will use anything he can to get us to violate this commandment, no matter how innocently it is packaged.

When we are desperate to change, Dr. Psycho's offerings are all the more tempting. Even psychologists can put us at risk of turning from the Super Power. In graduate school, I had a friend whose therapist convinced her she had "body memories" of sexual abuse by her father. My friend never remembers her father mistreating her, but the therapist stated that my friend's physical reaction to massage suggested it was the case. Of course, I can't say that my friend wasn't abused. But I can say God would not want us to seek life change through knowledge obtained in this way. The potential for destruction in my friend's life and her father's life was great.

God led the Israelites out of the slavery of Egypt into the desert. Moses went up on the mountain to talk to God and was gone a long time. The Israelites grew impatient and made a golden calf and worshiped it, believing it would get them out of their predicament. When we become impatient with God's timetable for life change, we are in danger of worshiping idols, too. The results for the Israelites were disastrous (Exodus 32).

We can overcome Dr. Psycho by:

Learning which practices and teachings God considers to be of the devil. Most Wonder Women who rely on astrology do not know God specifically forbids this in the Bible. To learn how to use the Bible, see Chapter 8, "Weapons of Change."

Waiting patiently for God to work change in us. The Israelites' golden calf didn't get them out of the desert any quicker than waiting on God. Our quick-fixes are likely to fail, too.

Praying for strength to stop idol-worshiping habits. The most powerful way to defeat Dr. Psycho is by calling an idol an idol. Refuse to use psycho babble and ask God to help you eliminate false gods (see Chapter 8).

Choosing counselors carefully. A good counselor, therapist, psychologist, psychiatrist, or doctor can be invaluable in making life changes. The best professionals believe in the Super Power and are in favor of using the weapons of change (Chapter 8). When finding a professional who believes as you do is difficult, be sure your counselor is willing to respect your faith.

DR. POISON

The comic Wonder Woman's list of adversaries includes Dr. Poison – a princess who uses chemical warfare on her intended victims. The thought of chemical warfare being used against us strikes fear in our hearts. We have visions of dirty bombs, poisoned water, and disease-ridden mail. We don't typically think of the chemical warfare being used against us every day.

I once met a friend in the emergency room where she was being treated for heart arrhythmias brought on by a weight loss medication. She thought she was having a heart attack. In my work as a drug trial coordinator and psychologist, I talked with many patients whose medications caused serious side effects such as seizures and ataxia (an inability to walk properly). Many times I have also had teachers and parents insist that a normal, active child be medicated for hyperactivity. We probably all know someone who's become dependent on medications that were supposed to heal them, not hurt them. Many of these cases are the handiwork of Dr. Poison.

Medications and medical treatments to aid us in changing have their place, but they also have their risks. There is no medication or herbal remedy that is risk-free. We risk losing money on useless treatments and our lives on dangerous ones. My research of quack medicine has given me serious concern about the unregulated use of herbal treatments, for example. But prescription medications are also dangerous. In our desperation to change, we may ignore potential side effects, take the poison, and suffer the consequences.

Even if a medication or treatment works without serious side effects, we may create an unnecessary dependency. For example, does a gastric bypass really make one lose weight? Or is it the change in eating habits? Is that anti-depressant really keeping you from "losing it" or do you relax more believing the med is handling things for you?

Dr. Poison's favorite concoction is Reverso – a mixture that makes people do the opposite of what they want. We take Reverso every time we use a medication or a surgery to take the place of the self-control we really desire. Friends who have taken anti-depressants complain that the drugs suppress the emotion that would normally motivate them to act. When taking Reverso, crises are viewed with an "Oh well" attitude. A Wonder Woman on Reverso is no Wonder Woman at all.

Please don't misunderstand me. I often recommend that truly anxious and depressed people take medication. Even if there is fear of dependency, short-term medication allows for the sleep, appetite, energy, and clearer thinking required to do the work of change. In such instances, a patient is not taking Reverso because she ultimately desires more self-control.

We can defeat Dr. Poison by:

Making sure a reputable and qualified professional recommends medication and/or treatment for the change we desire. For example, does your doctor want to know how you feel about medication before prescribing it?

Evaluating the risks including risks of dependency without thinking, "It can't happen to me."

Talking to those who have and have not used the medication or treatment we're considering. Would they use the same method again?

Giving a non-medical approach serious study and effort, unless a qualified professional feels it is inadvisable. For example, a suicidal person should usually take medication rather than trying self-help.

Watch for Dr. Poison and don't automatically fill her prescription.

HYPNOTA

This foe's name says it all. Hypnota hypnotizes others out of greed and a desire for personal gain.

I was fascinated by hypnosis as an undergraduate in psychology. I learned I had many misconceptions about it which you may share. First, hypnosis is not imposed upon another person against her will. Rather, all hypnosis is self-hypnosis. The brainwashing of torture victims may be an exception, but this kind of mind control isn't considered hypnosis.

Second, hypnosis cannot be used to coerce someone into doing something she wouldn't ordinarily do. For example, if a woman has put herself into a hypnotic state (often at the leading of a hypnotist), she will not commit murder. That is, unless she would have been willing to do so prior to being hypnotized.

Finally, hypnosis is not a magical state induced by incantations of which we're not aware. Rather, hypnosis is a relaxed state in which we are more open to suggestion – our own or someone else's.

Most of us experience states of hypnosis every day. Have you ever been so consumed in thought that you missed an exit as you were driving? Have you ever been so caught up in a book that you lost track of time? Have you ever watched television or a movie and found yourself so "into it" that you didn't hear someone trying to get your attention? These could all be considered hypnotic states.

With practice, hypnosis can be used to bring pain relief, reduce anxiety, and even control bleeding. Unfortunately, hypnosis hasn't been very successful (despite Hypnota's claims to the contrary) in reducing chronic addictions like smoking, drinking, or overeating. You may be out some money and still have your addiction if you choose hypnosis, but at least you will have learned to relax your body. This is an important skill for anyone to learn. The Bible frequently reminds us not to be afraid. Relaxation is simply training your body not to react with fear or anxiety when it isn't warranted. If a tornado is coming, however, fear and anxiety are warranted and will get you into the basement in time.

The problem with hypnosis, then, is not being in a relaxed state. It is that we are more accepting of what we hear and see. Wonder Women can use a relaxing hypnotic state to meditate on what is true. We'll discuss this in depth in Chapter 8, "Weapons of Change." Unfortunately, most of us do not spend our time in hypnotic states listening to or watching things that build us up. Rather, we allow Hypnota to make suggestions that tear us down.

Let's start with the television. The suggestions Hypnota makes are that clothes, cosmetics, surgery, teeth whitening, homes, cars, vacations, violence against our enemies, and sex outside of marriage will make us happy. That's just to name a few of her favorites. We often think we are immune to these suggestions, but we are not. TV shows, movies, and commercials are powerfully influential, in part because they work like hypnosis. We are relaxed and we hear the suggestions over and over and over.

Melanie became addicted to television as a young mother. First, she had to watch the same soap opera every day at the same time. She had no daily schedule, but by golly, she made sure she could watch "her show." The soap opera taught her no one could be trusted. Happiness was getting back together with your ex-husband who had cheated on you with your sister. Every day she watched she felt depressed, but she couldn't understand why.

As Wonder Woman, I gave up Melanie's soap operas, but Melanie remained addicted. When I read *The Plug-In Drug* by Marie Winn, I realized Melanie was letting her kids watch too much TV so she could have more time on the computer. While she surfed, she let her kids hypnotize themselves into believing reading was boring. Her two-year-old would scream if she didn't show him a movie. Meanwhile, he became so accustomed to passive communication, he couldn't speak.

When I set limits on TV time, Hypnota brought out the video games. *PlayStation Nation* gives a chilling description of young men who eschew taking on the world for getting to the next game level.[11] Video game characters joined Melanie's family and became the primary focus of conversation in her home. Her boys found playing in front of the screen more compelling than doing schoolwork, playing sports, and participating in family activities.

The worst result of Hypnota's television, computer, and video game trance was less time for Melanie to devote to change. I wanted Melanie and her family to spend more time together. I wanted her to spend more time writing. I wanted her to spend more time getting organized. But there she was in a spell. If we want to be victorious in the battle for change, we must wake up.

We can defeat Hypnota by:

Controlling the incantations. We want to be careful to screen what we are seeing and hearing in our media exposure. If what we're reading, watching or playing doesn't help us meet our goals, we have to make better choices. A digital video recorder allows me to make choices ahead of time about what my family and I will watch on TV.

Controlling trance time. Eliminating Hypnota completely is the easiest way to control trance time, but perhaps the toughest to implement. Getting rid of the television, video games, and the Internet is painful, but necessary for some of us. Most of us will choose to limit our trance time instead. Limit screen time to certain days or times. Use a timer and a partner to help hold you accountable. For example, promise the kids you'll play a game with them when your time is up and they'll be sure to keep you honest!

DEVASTATION

Devastation is a rival nearly identical to Wonder Woman. Yet her powers are used for evil, not good.

That word 'evil' often fools us. We often think evil is Hitler or Jeffrey Dahmer or Son of Sam – people we've never met and hopefully never will. Yet the Bible says, "So I find this law at work: When I want to do good, evil is right there with me" (Romans 7:21).

In *Spiderman 3*, Spiderman wants to do good. He wants to continue serving the people of his city and he wants to marry his high school sweetheart. But evil is right there with him. The attention he gets for being a superhero goes straight to his head and he stops paying attention to his girlfriend's needs. He also becomes obsessed with his uncle's murderer. As his desire for revenge grows, so does the size of his nemesis, the Sandman.

Spiderman's Devastation is Venom, a black suit that transforms him into an evil, powerful man. At first, Spiderman feels good wearing the armor of evil. Soon, however, he finds that it, like his anger, has become something he can't control.

Devastation for Wonder Women is our old self under Satanic control. The most frightening aspect of this particular enemy is our failure to recognize her. We believe we're Wonder Woman, getting the house in order, when we're really Devastation yelling at our families to shape up. We believe we're Wonder Woman, but we're really Devastation telling everyone it's "time to take care of me." We believe we're really Wonder Woman, but we're really Devastation spending money we don't have to solve our problems.

Spiderman finally realized he had to take off the black suit before it devastated him. It wasn't easy for him and it isn't easy for us to admit that pride, greed, laziness, or a desire for revenge is what is really driving our desire for change. But when we disrobe evil, we are ready to dress like the Wonder Women we are. Devastation is defeated when we know what to wear.

What to Wear

I still have my feet on the ground, I just wear better shoes.
Oprah Winfrey

I love the show, "What Not to Wear." The hosts evaluate the guest's lifestyle and goals and help them choose appropriate attire. Most of the guests bristle at seeing themselves on video and hearing the truth about their appearance. Most are also reluctant to try on a completely new style. They justify their reluctance by saying, "But these old clothes of mine are so comfortable!"

Your old self has gotten comfortable in her clothes, too. You may bristle at my suggestions for your Wonder Woman wardrobe, but I hope you will try on something new. Those who are made over on "What Not to Wear" are required to put their old clothes in the trash. Some of them pitch a fit about this part of the process, but do it. When they are supposed to shop for a completely different wardrobe, they often seek out new versions of the same-old, same-old. The hosts always intervene and strongly encourage the guests to stick with the new clothing rules.

Our Super Power has created an outfit befitting a Wonder Woman. But you may have a hard time letting go of your old clothes. At first, you may keep trying to recreate your old wardrobe. But once you really live in your new suit, I believe you, like every "What Not to Wear" makeover recipient, will wonder why you ever resisted the change.

On "What Not to Wear," potential guests are asked if they're willing to give up their old wardrobe for a brand new one. Willing participants are given a credit card with their name on it and a list of wardrobe rules. God isn't in the business of handing out credit cards, but He does give us "wardrobe rules" in the Bible. My Bible has my name engraved on it. Inside the Bible is Ephesians 6 which gives a list of what Wonder Women wear.

WARDROBE RULE #1: ...*with the belt of truth buckled around your waist*... (verse 14)

A Wonder Woman myth tells us the Amazon princess received her truth-producing lasso from a god. I remember a television Wonder Woman removing this lasso from her belt and wrapping it around crooks to force them to tell the truth.

Real Wonder Women have been given a belt of truth as a gift from the one and only God. It is wrapped around our waist so we might tell the truth, too. Jesus said, "If you hold to my teaching, you are really my disciples. Then you will know the truth, and the truth will set you free" (John 8:31b-32).

When we are open to learning and living God's ways, we are really His students. When we are His students, we know the truth, and the truth sets us free from anything that has overtaken our lives. Freedom comes from the truth.

When we find ourselves powerless to change, we are usually lying to ourselves and others. We'll say things like:

"I could quit anytime I wanted to. I just don't want to."
"I wouldn't have a problem if s/he would just…"
"It's not really a big deal."
"I can't change right now because…"

Even Melanie's small lies keep her in bondage. She likes to tell people she's late because she hits red lights or her kids can't find their shoes. The truth is she gets distracted by the computer and doesn't allow enough time to get where she's going.

Melanie had failed to lend something to one of her friends for several weeks. When she apologized to keep her friend from getting angry with her, her friend said, "That's okay. You have so many kids!" As Wonder Woman, I then chimed in and said, "Actually I was this way before I had any kids." Melanie's friend was astonished and said, "How very honest of you!"

The truth is what makes us extraordinary. Wrap your belt around your waist and tell yourself the truth about why you aren't changing. Is it really your hormones, your upbringing, and your circumstances? Or is it something else?

The Bible doesn't mention a skirt or pants, but we need more than just a belt of truth. Did you know that the first cartoon Wonder Woman actually wore a modest skirt? We don't have to put on a skimpy leotard to be a heroine. In fact, the Super Power admonishes us to be conservative in what we wear (1 Timothy 2:9). Not only do we want to be taken seriously, but we also want to keep others focused on our Super Power. Melanie prefers to dress like a Lynda-Carter Wonder Woman, complete with shiny bustier, so all eyes will be on her. But everything we Wonder Women wear should befit a lady of royal heritage.

WARDROBE RULE #2: ...*with the breastplate of righteousness in place*... (verse 14)

Do I have to tell you what WW's breastplate is? A Wonderbra of course. A bra is a godly uniform because it lifts us higher! The breastplate in a coat of armor protects the heart. The heart symbolizes love. Protecting the heart means keeping it from loving the wrong things or people. The Super Power wants us to love Him with our whole hearts (Matthew 22:37). When God doesn't have our hearts, His ability to teach us is diminished. When we seem unable to make lasting change, it is usually because we love something or someone more than we love God. The true test is how we react when the object of our affection is taken away.

If we become irritable/enraged or sad/depressed without our Internet time, chocolate, or spending money, for example, our affection may be in excess. We call this kind of desire for something having our hearts set on it. Like something set with Super Glue, once our hearts are set on having something or someone, the relationship is not easily ended. Our inner brat will end up kicking and screaming. She kicks to physically keep us from changing. As a result, we feel our energy levels drop without the sugar, caffeine, or cigarette to keep us going. Fatigue or illness keeps us from exercising.

But our inner brat isn't content to try to hold onto her Beloved with only a physical attack. She also screams for what she wants. The constant whining, justifying, guilting, complaining, and begging can really wear us down. Too often, to shut her up, we give her what she wants. But the quiet doesn't last long.

When Melanie was a girl, she foolishly touched her tongue to a frozen pole. Pulling the tongue away from a frozen pole is what it feels like when we break the connection between ourselves and something our hearts are set on. It hurts. We literally lose a part of ourselves in the process.

A nine-year-old Melanie and her seven-year-old brother spied some small animals in the barn. "Ooooo, they're rats!" her brother exclaimed. They were actually the stillborn pups of the family's St. Bernard, Dolly. The kids' father buried the pups, but the next day, Dolly had the pups with her on the front porch. She couldn't bear to give up her beloved pups. The kids' dad buried them deeper in the ground, but the next day Dolly had dug them up again. Finally, the pups were buried beneath a rubbish pile where poor Dolly wouldn't be able to smell them or get to them.

When we have our hearts set on something that we know isn't good for us, or if our affection for it is too great, we usually behave like Dolly. We don't want our idol to be "dead to us," even though our Super Power tells us death is the only way to be free from its power (Colossians 3:5). Because death is painful, we keep digging up our Beloved. We keep going back to the same guy. We keep shopping at the same mall. We keep going through the same drive-through.

There is no easy way to grieve. If we are cherishing anything more than God, breaking that bond will tear at our hearts like a knife. Hearts don't heal easily and any wounds can be fatal. That's why the Super Power tells us to guard our hearts so carefully.

I know more than one person whose heart was infected — even damaged — by bacteria that gained access through the mouth during dental work. Such small things are bacteria, but what great destruction they can do. To prevent infection, dentists will use antibiotics before treating an at-risk patient. We, too, have to be cautious about what our hearts are exposed to. Little things like TV shows, movies, books, and music can slowly infect us with a passion for the wrong things. We can prevent future heartache by setting limits on certain practices or taking a vacation from our Beloved to make sure we are not becoming dependent.

WARDROBE RULE #3: *...and with your feet fitted with the readiness that comes from the gospel of peace.* (Verse 13)

Melanie's doctoral research suggested that one's readiness for change before beginning treatment determined how much change patients actually made. To be ready for change, you have to wear the right shoes. Often times, you can determine what someone is going to do simply by looking at her shoes. Only a fool wears spike heels to hike or snowboots to dance.

Marla Cilley, author of *Sink Reflections*, strongly encourages women who want to create order in their homes to wear lace-up shoes every day. Wearing shoes, rather than slippers or sandals, tells our brains we're ready to work. If we're ready for change, we need to put on our Wonder Woman boots. You're going to be knee-deep in the mire even if a messy home isn't your problem. The boots are going to come in handy!

Remember when I said that another name for sin is miry or clayey? We all have a lot of filth to deal with because we are all sinners. The bad news is we can't be cleaned up until we admit we're stuck in the mud with no way out.

Our boots are to be made with the gospel. Gospel means good news and I have good news for you! God can get you out of the mess you're in when you have His boots on. Note that His boots are made of peace, not angry determination. Our old selves believe by directing their anger appropriately, they can get unstuck. The old gals think if we yell at ourselves and our families, everyone will know we mean business! Yet not even directing anger at our enemies will rescue us from the mud. Instead, anger has us thrashing about, entrenching us more deeply in sin than ever.

To be rescued from the muck and the mire, we need peace. Any lifeguard will tell you the danger of attempting to rescue a frantic person from drowning. Only when the potential drowning victim is at peace – holding still and trusting the rescuer – can she be saved. When we stop beating ourselves up, stop blaming others, and stop trying to

get unstuck, we can be rescued. We must admit we have a
problem that is bigger than we are. We must ask God and
those we have hurt as we've thrashed around for forgiveness.
When we do, God our Super Power will reach down with
His mighty right arm, pull us out of the mud, and set our feet
upon Jesus – the One the Bible calls a rock. Relying on His
strength, our feet will not slip (Psalm 121:3). We can enjoy
lasting freedom from the pit!

WARDROBE RULE #4: *In addition to all this, take up the shield
of faith, with which you can extinguish all the flaming arrows of the evil
one.* (Verse 16)

We wouldn't put on a nice suit and then drive down a
muddy road in a car with no windshield. We carry a shield of
faith to protect us from the lies that will be hurled our way as
we seek change. Lies like:

God is whoever you want him to be.
God can't help you. You have to help yourself.
You're a product of your genes and your environment.
You don't have what it takes to change.
The Bible isn't applicable to you today.

Have you been hit with any of these arrows? If so, your faith
in having a changed life has probably been wounded. Melanie
was hit by every single one of these arrows of falsehood, but
not me. As Wonder Woman I learned how to hold up my
shield of faith from Beth Moore's Bible study, *Believing God.* I

hold my hand in front of me, extending one finger as I recite each of the following five truths:

God is Who He says He is.
God can do what He says He can do.
I am who God says I am.
I can do all things through Christ.
God's Word is alive and active in me.

The shield of faith is taking God at His word. The rewards of carrying His shield are many, including:

Success (2 Chronicles 20:20)
Protection (Proverbs 2:8)
Forgiveness (Matthew 9:2)
Healing (Matthew 9:22)
Miracles (Matthew 21:21)
Sanctification; being made holy (Acts 26:18)
Obedience (Romans 1:5)
Salvation (1 Peter 1:9)
Pleasing God (Hebrews 11:6)

Our old selves carry a shield based on the enemy's lies. As much as we might like to, we cannot create a shield of faith. Only God can give us this shield as we hear the Good News about Jesus and His Word from the Bible (Ephesians 2:8-9; John 6:44; Romans 10:17). We don't need a big faith to see big changes in our lives (Luke 17:6). If we're lacking faith, we can ask God for it as a father of a demon-possessed boy did: "I do believe; help my unbelief" (Mark 9:24). The shield of faith works in concert with the weapons of change discussed in Chapter 8.

WARDROBE RULE #5: *Take the helmet of salvation* (Verse 17)

Wonder Woman's helmet is a crown. The helmet protects the head – a favorite target of the enemy. David, a shepherd boy, brought down the giant Goliath with a rock to the forehead – the most vulnerable part of him. Our helmet doesn't defend us from rocks, but protects us from attacks where we are most vulnerable – the mind.

There are many ways we can try to keep our thoughts under control. When we start to think of the chocolate chip cookie dough in the fridge, we can listen to music, make a phone call, or read a book. New Age teaching may have us repeating a mantra like "All is well" or "I'm at peace" to drive out offending thoughts. We may try counting or focusing on breathing to stay focused. But these methods of maintaining the "mind field" are destined to fail over time. What we need is the helmet of salvation.

We are dead in our sins. No amount of yoga or meditation will change that. But the helmet of salvation is a crown of life. When we receive Jesus as our Savior by faith, we become part of a royal family. We do not have to do anything to earn our helmets, but once we receive them, we will want to wear them.

Wearing the crown means we trust in the Super Power. We believe that God's Son, Jesus, died on the cross and was raised to life again so we, too, can be raised from the dead.

Wearing the crown means we believe there is life after the one we know on earth. We believe that one day we will live in heaven and will spend eternity there. Wearing the crown means we are living as Wonder Women.

The Bible tells us that the war between Flesh Woman and Wonder Woman will be waged in the mind (Romans 8:6). What difference does the helmet of salvation make in the battle? First, we know who wins. Flesh Woman, our old self, may have a few victories. We may yell at the kids, take the prescription pain killers we don't need, or leave the mess for another day. But the ultimate victory is Wonder Woman's through the Super Power.

Second, the helmet helps us think our way to victory. With salvation comes the Holy Spirit – the part of God who resides in us when we receive Jesus as our Savior. The Spirit teaches us to say no to what isn't right and He empowers us to do what is. The Bible says that those who live according to the sinful nature think about the things of the flesh. But those who live according to the spiritual nature think about spiritual things (Romans 8:5).

What does that mean? We are what we think (Proverbs 23:7). Cognitive-behavioral psychologists agree with this biblical truth. Flesh Woman thinks about her anniversary and the mop and bucket she received as a gift. These thoughts make her angry. Then she yells at her husband in front of the kids – something she wants to change. Wonder Woman, with her helmet on, thinks about her anniversary. She remembers the mop and bucket. She remembers, too, that her husband was apologetic. She remembers how her husband forgave her when she backed into the neighbor's car. She remembers how God forgave her for countless times she was thoughtless. Then she forgives her husband.

The helmet of salvation helps us remember we are princesses who will live in a kingdom with no end. No food or gadget or relationship can compare to what the Super Power has prepared for us (1 Corinthians 2:9). But to think like Wonder Woman, we must think about "whatever is true, whatever is noble, whatever is right, whatever is pure, whatever is lovely, whatever is admirable—if anything is excellent or praiseworthy—think about such things" (Philippians 4:8). Our inner brat doesn't want us to think about these things, so she will keep bringing up her topics of choice.

I once drove two hours of a ten-hour trip with two young children in the back. At that point I began to feel queasy. I figured it was just gas or something and chuckled to myself as I wondered what someone in my position would do if they had the stomach flu. I would soon find out. As I continued driving with severe nausea, I tried to focus my mind on anything but how sick I felt. The brats, I mean kids, in the back kept screaming for cookies and ice cream. No matter how much I begged them not to use food words, they continued to torment me. My helmet didn't keep me from getting sick that day, but it did encourage me to know I would soon be home.

Our helmets encourage all of us in knowing we will soon be home. The troubles we are now experiencing are thankfully temporary (2 Corinthians 4:18). Although the battle for change will last a lifetime, our present circumstances won't. I often reassure myself in the midst of a tense movie that a happy ending is coming. When we believe in the Super Power and trust in Jesus, we can reassure ourselves with hope for a happy ending, too.

The helmet can protect our thoughts, but we need weapons to win the battle for our minds. We'll take up arms in the next chapter.

Weapons of Change

God has handed us two sticks of dynamite with which to demolish our strongholds: His Word and prayer.
Beth Moore, *Praying God's Word Day by Day*

Once we're dressed in our Wonder Woman suits, we are ready to learn to use the weapons of change. I don't recall the cartoon Wonder Woman carrying a sword, but real Wonder Women do. Ephesians 6:17 says, "…and the sword of the Spirit, which is the word of God."

WHY THE SWORD?

Melanie once worked alone at a sub sandwich shop until three in the morning. One evening, a drunk threatened to jump the counter to have his way with her. Melanie picked up the large knife she used for cutting sandwiches and confidently advised against it. The man quickly left the store.

Our Wonder Woman swords, like the sandwich knife, will cause our enemy to turn around and run. Without a weapon, we are vulnerable to attack in the battlefield of our minds. But even if we own a weapon, we are sure to be defeated if we don't use it.

Melanie owned a sword all her life, but had never spent more than a few minutes using it. She thought of the Bible like a dictionary. If she needed to look something up, she would. But read it? That seemed crazy! Besides, she thought she knew what was in that book. She'd heard the great Bible stories about Noah and the ark, David and Goliath, Jonah and the whale. The rest was a bunch of begats and thou-shalt-nots that didn't seem to have anything to do with her life.

In college, Melanie was taught that the Bible was a book written by imperfect men. As such, it contained errors. She also learned that the Bible's instructions were for an ancient culture. Much of it, she was told, was not meant to be taken literally. It contained stories that were merely being used to suggest a moral approach to living. Evolution was taught as fact. As a result of her education, Melanie believed in a creator God and evolution. She didn't know how creation and evolution fit together, but figured it didn't really matter.

A week before her second child was due, Melanie attended a seminar on changing your life with Becky Tirabassi. At the time, a changed life was exactly what she was looking for. She no longer had roach roommates, but she was still overwhelmed by parenting, household chores, and other responsibilities. Becky shared how she had been stuck in alcoholism and promiscuity when a janitor at a church told her about the Good News. Becky's life was forever changed when, through Jesus, she became connected to the Super Power. She was so elated to have God's power in her life, she became committed to connecting with Him and reading His Word, the Bible, daily.

During the seminar, Becky asked for commitments to daily appointments with the King using the sword. I stood up ready to commit. I was nervous because Melanie had never been very good at keeping commitments. But with high hopes, I took home my *Change Your Life Daily Bible*, written in plain language. The next morning, I grasped my sword, opened this manual for wonderful living, and read. I read the next day and the next day and the next. I was so inspired and excited by what I read in those pages that I was also sad I had left such a treasure gathering dust on my bookshelf. In the Bible I found wisdom and power for becoming the heroine I wanted to be.

I found the Bible was not just a family history book and not just a book for wisdom, but also a book of letters from a Father.

My father wasn't a big talker. Although I loved him, I didn't feel close to my dad growing up. He didn't tell me much about himself nor did he talk much about his hopes for me. When I left home for college, things changed. My father began to write me letters. The letters told me who my dad was and what was important to him. I felt assured of his love for me and as a result, I felt closer to him than I ever had. I can't imagine not reading Dad's letters. What riches I would have missed!

Our heavenly Father has written us letters, too, my dear Sister. Maybe God has always seemed distant to you. Perhaps you've wondered if you could really know Him. Maybe you've believed He doesn't really care for you at all. Reading His letters to you in the Bible can help you know Him and love Him and be assured of his deep love for you. The Holy Spirit in us can make the words of these letters come to life, as though God Himself were speaking to us in the moment (Hebrews 4:12).

One night I was in the midst of a night terror when I was sure someone was going to break into my home. I prayed for peace and opened my Bible randomly and this is what I read:

> I love you, O LORD, my strength. The LORD is my rock, my fortress and my deliverer; my God is my rock, in whom I take refuge. He is my shield and the horn of my salvation, my stronghold. I call to the LORD, who is worthy of praise, and I am saved from my enemies (Psalm 18:1-3).

Another night I received word that my father was near death. I was so distraught and cried out to the Lord that I wasn't ready for Dad to leave this world. I asked God to give me some assurance that He had heard my prayer. I opened the Bible randomly once again and this is what I read:

> No one remembers you when he is dead. Who praises you from the grave? I am worn out from groaning; all night long I flood my bed with weeping and drench my couch with tears. My eyes grow weak with sorrow; they fail because of all my foes. Away from me, all you who do evil, for the LORD has heard my weeping. The LORD has heard my cry for mercy; the LORD accepts my prayer (Psalm 6:5-9).

The words gave me assurance that God heard my prayer and my father would recover. He did.

Years later I had three sons and was expecting a fourth baby. I wondered if a fourth son or a first daughter would be joining our family. An online friend mentioned she prayed for the gender of her unborn child to be revealed to her. That night her son dreamt his mother was carrying a sister. She was indeed.

I wondered if God might also reveal my child's gender to me. I prayed He would tell me the gender in His Word if it was His will that I would know. I opened my daily Bible to the date of my scheduled ultrasound and read:

And as she was having great difficulty in childbirth, the midwife said to her, "Don't be afraid, for you have another son" (Genesis 35:17).

I thought I could have misunderstood because there aren't many passages of the Bible that talk about daughters, but sure enough the ultrasound technician confirmed I was having my fourth son. The evening of my ultrasound I went out to dinner with the women in my Bible study group to celebrate learning our baby's gender. My friends had hoped I would have a daughter, but had a lot of fun discussing what they thought this baby's name should be. After much discussion and debate, the group concluded his name should be Benjamin.

When I came home, I looked up Genesis 35:17, the passage in which God gave me the baby's gender. The son referred to was given the name Benjamin. I am convinced God speaks to us through the Bible, directly and personally, just as any living father would. But before you are equally convinced, you will want to know God has really written these letters.

I completed a Bible study called *God's Amazing Book* that gave me total confidence in God as the Bible's author. I reprint a paragraph of that study here:

> The word Bible simply means "book." But this is no ordinary book. It has appealed to people from every tribe and nation throughout the ages. Historically, it is a runaway for the prize of the best-seller ever written. And it is a book that does not just captivate the reader; it has a powerful potential for actually changing the reader. No other book has so affected individuals and transformed societies. The Bible is actually a collection of 66 books, written over a span of more than 1500 years, with at least 40 different authors from different countries, social strata, and occupations. Yet this book has a unity and cohesiveness that leave an open-minded, discerning person with only one logical explanation: God is the true author of this book.[12]

The Bible itself proclaims God as its author: "All Scripture is God-breathed and is useful for teaching, rebuking, correcting and training in righteousness" (2 Tim 3:16). Jesus Himself quoted the Bible: "It is written in the Prophets: 'They will all be taught by God.' Everyone who listens to the Father and learns from him comes to me" (John 6:45). Melanie's college professors wanted her to believe the Bible contained errors and untruths because it was written by imperfect people. But the Bible wasn't written by ordinary men. Rather, it was written by Supermen empowered by the Holy Spirit (2 Peter 1:21; 1 Thessalonians 2:13).

When I watched a video on dinosaurs and the Bible by Answers in Genesis, I learned I could believe all of the Bible – even the stories that seemed like fairy tales.[13] The scientific evidence doesn't contradict the Bible; only some scientists do. The Bible tells us that all the major kinds of animals were created on the same day that man was. Man and dinosaur lived together. Scientists who believe we are the result of inter-species evolution, however, believe dinosaurs and other prehistoric beasts were extinct for millions of years before man evolved into being.

Shortly after watching the Answers in Genesis video, my children and I went to a museum with fossils of mastodons. The video the museum showed acknowledged that archeologists were shocked to discover a mastodon fossil with an arrow head embedded in it. Clearly man and this "prehistoric" animal had dwelt together. Scientists scrambled to revise their theories about the mastodon's history, but those who believe the Bible have no difficulties with such evidence.

As Wonder Women, we won't use a sword we know is faulty. If we believe the Bible is weak, we'll look for what we think are more powerful weapons, like psychology, biology, or astrology. The problem with these weapons is they constantly change. The Bible doesn't change. The *God's Amazing Book* Bible study I completed gave me confidence in that:

Then in 1947 the Dead Sea scrolls were discovered. These scrolls dating from the first to the second century

B.C., included portions of every Old Testament book but Esther. They remarkably demonstrated the accuracy of transmission of copies through all of those centuries. What a strong reminder that God has overseen the formation and preservation of His Word![14]

Using the Bible as a plumb line results in consistent living that will never fail. Like a knight with his "trusty sword," we must believe in the power of the sword so we will choose to battle with it every time.

CHOOSE YOUR SWORD

When you are ready to wield a sword, you may be confused about which one to choose. There are many different versions. If you are completely new to the Bible, I recommend a couple of different approaches.

First, you may choose to read the Bible through in a year using a dated daily Bible. The *Change Your Life Daily Bible*[15] is written in contemporary language and includes a passage of the Old Testament (the story of God's people before Jesus came), the New Testament (the story of Jesus and His church), Psalms (songs or poems written in praise of God), and Proverbs (a book of wisdom). Reading just fifteen minutes a day from different parts of the Bible can keep you from getting stuck in books that are less interesting (e.g., Leviticus).

The drawback of dated daily Bibles is potential discouragement if you miss a day or two and have trouble catching up. If you want to read an undated Bible in a year, you can find a reading plan at www.bibleplan.org. Another good alternative is to have daily Bible readings sent to your email address. With www.bibleinayear.org, you can choose the version you prefer to read. NIV (for New International Version) is the preferred version for most Bible studies, but not all.

A second potential approach to reading the Bible is to read it chronologically. Chronological Bibles group passages that occur at the same time, regardless of which Bible book they are in. They read more like a story book. *The Narrated Bible* by F. LaGard Smith is a chronological Bible with commentary that can give you some insight into what you are reading. This Bible can be read in a year, too, but the daily readings aren't dated. This approach to reading in a year makes it easy for perfectionists to stay motivated even when they're forced to miss days. The website www.bibleplan.org will give you a yearly chronological plan that can be used with any Bible.

A third potential approach is to read passages that apply to your desired change. Most Bibles have what's called a concordance in the back that will list passages by word. If you are looking for help with anger, you could look under the words anger, rage, and wrath, for example. You can also do a word or topic search electronically. Bible software, hand-held electronic Bibles, and the Internet make it simple to find verses that address your needs.[16] You may also choose one of several Bibles written for specific audiences. For example, you may like the *NIV Recovery Devotional Bible* by Verne Becker or the *Women of Faith Devotional Bible* by Patsy Clairmont, Luci Swindoll, and Sheila Walsh. These

Bibles' devotionals include short readings that personalize the Bible using stories or examples.

Finally, you could use the Quick Start approach. To get familiar with your sword quickly, you may wish to read Genesis and the book of John. You can locate these books via the table of contents in the front of your Bible. Abbreviations such as 1 Tim. always refer to the book of the Bible. The first number in a Scripture citation refers to the chapter and the number following the colon indicates the verse(s) within that chapter.

If you are experienced with the sword, perhaps you would benefit from a new one. Try a different version of the Bible, read a paraphrase like *The Message*, or follow one of the other recommendations I've given in this section.

TRAINING WITH THE SWORD

Owning a sword is a bit like using a computer. It isn't enough to get your computer set up and plugged in. You need instruction to get the most out of it. You could teach yourself using manuals and tutorials, but the quickest way to learn is hands-on training with an experienced teacher. Wonder Women call hands-on training with the sword "Bible study." Someone who wants to become truly skilled in sword fighting knows there will be a certain amount of hard work involved. Training won't be all fun and games. So it is with Bible study.

It takes practice to look up verses quickly and to understand their context and meaning. It takes time to read the Word and attend classes, but the rewards of being able to defend yourself in the battle for the mind are well worth the effort. The better you get at studying the Bible, the more you'll enjoy it.

You can train with your sword by yourself at home and you should! There are many Bible studies that can help you to comprehend and apply what you read to your life. You can watch or listen to Bible teachers who can facilitate your learning. Numerous tools are available to help you in your studies, such as a Bible handbook, commentaries, a complete concordance, and a Bible dictionary. Software programs and Bible websites provide these tools in one place. Using these references, advanced Wonder Women can gain great insight into a problem area by reading applicable verses, meanings of key words in Greek or Hebrew, and commentaries on passages that are particularly relevant.

Studying the sword is of great value to the swordswoman, but training must be so thorough that it is second nature. To win the battle for the mind, we need the mind of the Super Power (1 Corinthians 2:16). To have His mind, we need His words. To have His words in mind, we must meditate on them until they are committed to memory.

For many years I struggled to memorize Bible verses I knew would change my thinking, my emotions, and my behavior in a positive way. Then I discovered Memlok.[17] This computer- and business-card based program uses pictures and short, but regular review periods to help you keep verses in long-term memory.

For example, Joshua 1:8 says: "Do not let this Book of the Law depart from your mouth; meditate on it day and night, so that you may be careful to do everything written in it. Then you will be prosperous and successful." The picture you see on your computer screen (or on a printed business card) is of a donut with the word LET written on it. When you see the picture, you'll think "Donut let" and you'll likely recall the rest of the verse.

Memlok allows you to choose verses by category so you can focus your attention on verses that apply to the change you desire. There are other Scripture memory programs available and you could design your own. The key to the success of any system is using it regularly.

There is much training we Wonder Women can do on our own, but we benefit greatly from participating in group studies. We need our Wonder Sisters to keep our sword and our skills sharp (Proverbs 27:17). Studying in a class means we can profit from the teaching of an experienced teacher in person or via video made more affordable by the group. Group study's built-in accountability makes it easier to practice with the sword regularly. Studying with others means we benefit from diverse opinions and experiences. The environment is also perfect for making close friendships.

But group Bible study can be scary for many reasons. The small group may bring up old fears of rejection. We may fear getting close and then being hurt. We may fear having our confidences shared with others. We may fear that our lack of Bible knowledge, our poor reading skills, or our lifestyle will cause us embarrassment.

These fears are not completely unfounded. We do put ourselves at risk when we join any group. Should we participate in a group that treats us poorly, we should quickly get out of it. One bad group doesn't mean there are no good ones. I have been deeply hurt by collective study, but I have been greatly rewarded by it, too. As in all relationships, the risk is worth the reward.

THE WEAPON OF PRAYER

The fantasy Wonder Woman was given gold bracelets to defend herself from her enemies' bullets. She spent much time training herself in the use of the bracelets because she knew they were vitally important in battle. When we Wonder Women put our bracelets on, we bring them together to defend ourselves with another vitally important weapon: prayer. Ephesians 6:18 tells us: "And pray in the Spirit on all occasions with all kinds of prayers and requests."

Melanie thought prayer meant saying, "Now I lay me down to sleep…" when she was a child or saying "Thank you, God" before holiday meals. She thought it was what you did when you were in deep trouble. She didn't know it was the way she communicated with the Super Power. She didn't know that the power to change required constant communication.

Melanie's first major lesson in prayer was learned in the Soviet Union. Melanie traveled to the U.S.S.R. as part of a college seminar studying Eastern vs. Western psychology. Melanie knew she had trouble losing things. Her worst nightmare was losing her passport and valuables in a foreign country.

On the plane to England during the first leg of the trip, Melanie awoke and knew she had misplaced something valuable. She began digging through her belongings, frantically trying to find the missing item. Her seatmate noticed her distress and began helping her look. The seatmate enlisted the assistance of the other students in the row, and then asked Melanie for a description of the lost item. When Melanie mutely gestured nonsensically in the air, they both realized she'd just had a nightmare.

Melanie awakened to a real nightmare just days later. The group traveled from Leningrad to Moscow by train overnight. The students were advised to wear their passports and valuables as they slept to prevent theft. When Melanie was awakened early in Moscow, she quickly searched her bed, grabbed her luggage and got off the train. When she arrived at the small ship that would be her hotel room an hour later, she was asked to turn in her passport with the other students. At that moment, she knew her passport had been left in the bedding on the train.

Melanie's passport, visa, credit card, airplane tickets, and half her cash were in the pouch that had been left behind. The seminar leader explained to Melanie that the group would not be able to wait for her while she obtained a new passport and visa. The group's co-leader told her that her passport had likely been sold on the black market and a phone call home would be more than she or her family could afford.

Melanie didn't get upset or cry at all. Until she was alone in her room – then she fell apart. She had never been more terrified. She had never felt more helpless. She was in a fox hole and she was ready to pray. Her admission of helplessness allowed me, Wonder Woman, to take over. I remembered hearing once that you should pray until you felt at peace. I began praying specifically that whoever found my passport would turn it in. I prayed and prayed and prayed until I felt peace. Strangely, once that peace came, I felt completely confident that my passport would be returned. I was so confident that I easily fell asleep. I was awakened at midnight by my seminar leader who told me my passport pouch had been recovered. I was not surprised to find that not one thing had been removed from it.

WHY PRAY?

Melanie should have understood the power of prayer after that dramatic rescue, but she kept forgetting. When she attended the Becky Tirabassi seminar on life change, she was reminded of the necessity of prayer. Becky told story after story of answered prayer. She said she prayed and felt God's assurance that she would sell her house in one day. She and her husband had an open house for their home and at the end of it, no one had made them an offer. She still felt God had given her the message that her home would sell in just one day. Later that evening, a couple arrived who felt compelled to see the house despite the fact the open house was over. The couple bought it and Becky's prayer was answered.

Adrian Rogers shared a similar story on his radio broadcast.[18] He said his car broke down one night in the rain. He prayed and felt the Lord's assurance that the first car that came by would stop to help. Adrian saw that first car pass him by. He was discouraged. He wondered if he had misunderstood God. He wondered if he would have to walk!

Eventually a car did stop to provide assistance. It was the first car who passed him originally come back to help.

George Mueller was a 19th century man of prayer. He was traveling by ship to do a speaking engagement. The captain informed George that bad weather would require him to miss his engagement. George informed the captain that he had never been late and didn't expect to be this time either. The captain insisted there was nothing he could do. George prayed for a change in weather so he could arrive on time. God answered that prayer and the captain put his faith in Jesus.[19]

When we don't pray, it's often because we're focusing on the how of praying rather than the why. We pray because God asks us to pray, but mostly we pray because prayer works. Prayer releases the power of God in our lives. I believe that next to the helmet of salvation, the bracelets of prayer are the most powerful weapon we have in the battle for change.

True stories of answered prayer will remind us of the truth of James 4:2: We do not have because we do not ask. If you have not experienced the life change you desire, prayer is the answer. Youth With a Mission's *Christian Heroes: Then & Now* series of biographies will inspire you with tales of answered prayer in the lives of ordinary men and women who serve a supernatural God. Becky Tirabassi also suggests recording our own answers to prayer so will be continually inspired to pray.

HOW TO PRAY

Jesus' students (called disciples) asked Him how they should pray. He answered them by giving what we now call the Lord's Prayer:

> Our Father in heaven, hallowed be your name, your kingdom come, your will be done on earth as it is in heaven. Give us today our daily bread. Forgive us our debts, as we also have forgiven our debtors. And lead us not into temptation, but deliver us from the evil one (Matthew 6:9-13).

The prayer wasn't given as the only prayer we should recite, but as a model of a perfect prayer, say theologians. We can benefit from using a formula for our prayers, like the acronym, P.R.A.Y.

First we Praise. We tell God all of His character traits we appreciate and thank Him for His goodness to us. I often like to read one of the psalms out loud so I am not just praising Him for what He does, but also for who He is.

Second, we Repent. We admit our mistakes, our willful disobedience, and even our wrong thoughts. We tell God we do not want to rebel against Him again.

Third, we Ask. This is when we make requests for ourselves and others.

Finally, we yield. We listen for God's response. We may receive it immediately in our spirit, through His Word, or sometime later.

Becky Tirabassi's *Let Prayer Change Your Life* describes the approach to prayer I used for many years – an approach you may enjoy, too. Using a prayer journal (just a 3-ring binder with tabbed sections), I wrote out my prayers. What I like about writing prayers is less interference from distracting thoughts. I can record prayer requests as I receive them and the answers, too. I have a record of God's work in my own and others' lives. Today my prayer journal is one section of my Creative Planner that I will describe in Chapter 9, "Winging It."

Whether we speak, write, or silently pray and whether we use a journal, prayer software, or nothing at all to organize our prayer lives, we should pray this way:

Relationally (Matthew 6:9). Jesus calls God "Father." I didn't realize until I read Nancy Leigh DeMoss's *A Place of Quiet Rest* that I had been speaking to God as though he were an electronic operator. My speech was stilted and awkward. Because my dad and I weren't close until the last few years of his life, I didn't know what a father-daughter relationship was supposed to look like. I was pretty sure it wasn't memorized scripted material, however. I have been freed to enjoy communicating with God the way I would with a beloved father. I talk. He listens. He talks. I listen.

Continuously (1 Thessalonians 5:17). Although a time reserved specifically for prayer is valuable, we can pray anytime, anywhere, anyhow. A prayer for peace can help us keep our wits with the screaming toddler in the car.

Praying on the phone with someone in need will keep us from forgetting later. Praying for help with temptations, decisions, and frustrations can take up a good portion of our day.

Broadly (Ephesians 6:18). No request is inconsequential to God. A new stove, a new dress, and a new idea are all requests that have been granted to me or to other Wonder Sisters I know.

Humbly (Luke 11:2, Matthew 26:42; Matthew 6:5). We pray without drawing attention to ourselves for God's will to be done. In *Spiderman 3*, a man enters a church and prays for Peter Parker to die. I could have told him his request wouldn't be granted! If we ask for what we know God doesn't want, we're wasting our breath. I often make my request and ask God to change my heart if the request cannot be granted.

Confidently (Mark 11:24). We must have faith when we pray. But having faith is difficult when we know God may refuse our request. Believing prayer isn't blindly assuming we'll get what we want. Believing prayer is trusting that God is able to do anything in Jesus' name. Believing prayer is trusting that God will do what He says He will do. If we have peace or a Word from the Super Power confirming His answer to prayer, we must hold fast to our faith and ask Him to strengthen us in it.

Persistently (Luke 18:1-8). Jesus told a story of a widow who banged on a judge's door repeatedly asking for justice. The judge who was evil granted her request, just to stop her harassment. Jesus said a just God will do likewise, not begrudgingly, but graciously. We cannot give up even if we must make the same appeal for years.

Privately (Mark 1:35; Matthew 6:6). There are many benefits of time spent alone in prayer, but the greatest is hearing God speak to us. I don't hear voices. Well, maybe I do. I hear a voice in my head sometimes that sounds like me, but I know is the Holy Spirit. I have "heard" Him as I am going about my day. I have heard Him in books, movies, radio, and in others' counsel. But most often I hear Him when I am alone with Him in the quiet.

Communally (Acts 12:5). I recently used an approach to group prayer advocated by Denise Glenn of Motherwise.[20] In small groups of five or six, each mother prayed a sentence prayer over each request. Hearing everyone in my group pray for me often brought me to tears and the requests were granted more often than for any other approach I've used. Acts 12 tells the story of Peter being miraculously released from prison when the church prayed. Miracles happen for those in various kinds of "prisons" when we agree together in prayer.

Empathically (1 Timothy 2:1; 1 Corinthians 10:13). I am indebted to Janice McBride for her suggestion of praying for those who are being seized by the same temptations we are.[9] We are not the only women who have a hard time with self-discipline. We are not the only women struggling with a difficult relationship. So when we are in the heat of battle, we must remember to pray not only for ourselves, but for those facing the same circumstances.

Scripturally (Luke 23:46; Psalm 31:6). Beth Moore taught me the power of praying God's Word. Although I believe silent prayers are heard by the Super Power, there's something about speaking His Words out loud. In her video Bible study, *Believing God*, Beth says praying this way "sounds like God to the devil." Her books, *Praying God's Word Day by Day* and *Praying God's Word: Breaking Free From Spiritual Strongholds* have given me a place to look for Bible verses I can pray for my needs.

Defiantly (Matthew 5: 44). Satan wants us to pray for our enemies to be cursed; God wants us to pray for their blessing. We can defy the enemy of our souls by asking God to turn our adversaries into fellow superheroes. Our prayerful obedience will bless us, too.

The book you are holding in your hands would not exist if not for prayer. My prayer has been that this book might introduce you to the life-changing love of the Super Power. If you would like personal prayer, please submit your prayer request to www.prayforyou.org.

Winging It

He who loves flies and rejoices; he is free and nothing holds him back.

Henri Matisse

Despite Edna's warnings of the dangers of capes in *The Incredibles* movie, Wonder Women wear capes. They remind us we were created to fly.

Although the Super Power had taken control of Melanie's eating and exercise habits, Melanie still reigned supreme when it came to home organization. The roaches had never returned, but there were plenty of things that still bugged her.

With three children ages three and under, the laundry was more than Melanie could manage. She usually forgot it was in the washer. By the time she remembered it, she had to wash it twice to remove the musty smell. The laundry in the dryer typically sat so long, it required ironing. Ironing, on the rare occasions it was done, was completed in a panic when getting ready for church. Laundry to be folded was thrown on the unmade bed. In the evenings, her husband grumbled about not being able to get to bed because of the laundry baskets. In the mornings, he grumbled about not being able to find clean clothes.

Laundry and dishes and cleaning were usually done in response to one of her husband's fits or because Melanie was having company and didn't want to be embarrassed. Whenever the couple entertained, Melanie picked up everything and threw it into the closets and the basement. "Everything" included mail and important papers. When Melanie got around to sorting through the piles, she usually discovered unpaid bills and missed appointment slips.

Company-panic cleaning was one reason Melanie had clutter; mystery shopping was another. Whenever Melanie needed something, she bought it, even though she knew she already owned it. She didn't want to take the time to solve the mystery of where she'd put the needed items. This is how she accumulated enough office and craft supplies to run a school. A third reason for the piles was her penchant for saving. Melanie saved gifts she didn't like because she didn't want to hurt anyone's feelings. She saved craft materials because someday she would have time to create. She saved books and papers because someday someone might need them. All of her saving was costing her time and money.

A housekeeper was an obvious solution. Melanie figured she would be too ashamed to leave the house a mess for a housekeeper, so not only would the house be picked up, but it would be clean, too! The plan worked just as she hoped for a few weeks. But before long, she felt more and more comfortable with the housekeeper seeing the mess. It took longer and longer for the housekeeper to clean as she had to pick up, too.

Around the same time, Melanie had begun homeschooling her oldest child for preschool as a test for herself. She wondered if she had what it took to teach elementary school to her children. She was failing the test miserably. The school day never started at the same time and was constantly interrupted by the phone and by inattentiveness – Melanie's. Although Melanie longed for organized housekeeping and homeschooling, she started to believe it was another fairy tale to forget.

When Melanie was hired to write a booklet on life balance, she started looking for a "happily ever after" to her disorganized tale. She followed the yellow brick road to www.FLYLady.net on a friend's recommendation. Melanie was immediately drawn to the FLYLady's down-to-earth style. FLYLady freely admitted she had been every bit the mess that Melanie was. FLYLady, also known as Marla Cilley, once had a home so cluttered that police officers responding to a neighbor's emergency pulled their guns, believing her home had been ransacked. Marla discovered how to live clutter-free, one baby step at a time, and began sharing her wisdom with women online.

The FLYLady philosophy was that women who struggled with organization were SHEs (Sidetracked Home Executives). Melanie was familiar with this concept from reading *The Sidetracked Sisters' Happiness File* by Pam Young & Peggy Jones. The two sisters described their distractibility and explained how an index card file with a daily schedule had changed their lives. Melanie still had the card file, but she'd never gotten past the "create a daily schedule" task because she couldn't come up with a perfect schedule that fit every day.

FLYLady seemed to understand what made Melanie tick. She wrote that perfectionism is what kept people from cleaning daily. To undo wrong thinking and bad habits, FLYLady sent daily "FLYwashing" emails, testimonials, and task reminders. Rather than scheduling, FLYLady recommended routines – a set of tasks done in the same order over and over until they became reflexive. At first, Melanie copied FLYLady's routines so she didn't have to come up with the perfect ones. Somewhere in the midst of the FLY-t training, I found I was Wonder Woman FLYing free, leaving Melanie in the dust.

FLY IS FINALLY LOVING YOURSELF

Marla Cilley says an online subscriber dubbed her the FLYLady because she is an avid fly fisherman. FLY became the acronym for Finally Loving Yourself. Marla had experienced self-loathing in her messy, chaotic life as an abused wife. Loving herself is what helped free her of clutter and disorganization. I had seen Melanie berate herself every time she lost something, overslept, or let the house go. But I had never seen it do any good. Melanie felt like an unlovable failure.

Love is what gave me wings – love for my old slobby self, love for my husband, love for my children, love for my home, and love for the Super Power. I learned self-love isn't what Melanie thought it was: ice cream when she wasn't hungry, hours in front of the computer, spending money on books and crafts. *Christ Esteem* by Don Matzat points out that self-esteem in the traditional sense simply isn't possible because we know how bad we can be. I certainly knew how bad Melanie could be! I needed a concept of loving myself that went beyond self-indulgence and hollow affirmations. I found it in the Word of God:

> Be imitators of God, therefore, as dearly loved children and live a life of love, just as Christ loved us and gave himself up for us as a fragrant offering and sacrifice to God (Ephesians 5:1-3)

I understood loving children dearly. I was crazy about the three I had when I found FLYlady. What I didn't understand was that God loved me as much and more. I didn't stop loving my children when they didn't put their toys away. I didn't stop loving my children when they forgot to do something. I didn't stop loving my children when they whined. God hadn't stopped loving me. God's love for me made it possible for me to love without conditions, too. I could forgive my inner brat, my husband, and my children because I had been forgiven. My Wonder Sister, our Super Power God loves you dearly. When we whirl around and want to do things His way, the old things are forgotten (Isaiah 43:25).

I learned a new definition of love: sacrifice. Loving myself didn't mean indulgence. It meant being willing to give up habits and things that weren't God's best for me: phone marathon sessions, lots of outside activities, hours online. Loving myself also meant being willing to say yes to things that were hard: requiring the kids to do chores, picking up when tired, getting up early.

I began to see that pursuing order in my life was how I could love myself and my family. FLYLady helped. She called the weekly cleaning routine the "Home Blessing." I discovered that changing sheets, dusting, and vacuuming are all ways that I can bless my home and my family. Funny how the words we use can completely change our attitudes!

Fortunately, love didn't require me to work alone. Teaching my children to help is also blessing them. Laurie Flem, founder of *TEACH* magazine, says she was embarrassed she had to pay others to do her laundry at college, because she'd never learned at home. She called her mother and told her she needed to teach her younger sisters to do their own laundry to save them from the same fate. Soon, her younger sister called her, angry for the extra work. Learning to work is a blessing even if our young students don't agree!

A dear friend helped me see the blessing in my husband's housekeeping habits. She shared with a group of engaged couples that she was constantly annoyed by her husband's propensity for not putting some of his clothing away. Then she realized she would never have to put the clothing away again if her husband were gone.

One homeschooling mother lives that reality. For an online support group, she wrote of her experience and I reprint it here with her permission:

> In two weeks it will be three years since my husband died. I miss him so very much. It still hurts so very much... I am tired. I am tired of not having my other half. I am tired of making all the decisions...

I miss his touch. I miss his smile. I miss his whiskers in the sink. I miss his towel in the bathroom. I miss his car. I miss his Bible lessons and history lessons. I miss our trips. I miss his awful cooking. I miss his laid back personality. I miss the balance he gave me. I miss drying his hair and trimming his moustache. I miss his mud boots and work jacket at the door. I miss the sound of his chain saw as he butchers another poor bush in the yard.

…I miss his smell…I miss his clothes in the wash. I miss his stinky socks. I miss typing for him. I miss trying to figure out his horrible handwriting. I miss the dirt when they came home from camping…I miss straightening his tie, picking his clothes because he never could match anything.

Please do not ever take your husband for granted. Michael was gone in a flash and there is so much I wish I could have said and could have done before he went to be with the Lord. No matter how much or how little they do, be thankful every day. When they frustrate you and make you mad, thank God you have that. I would do anything to have him back. Go find your dh [dear husband] and tell him you love him and are so glad you have him. Then go thank God for your dh.

Love makes it easy to FLY. But if you'd rather clean a county's worth of toilets than love your husband, you may find some help in Chapter 11, "Winning with Superman."

TIME

Brats want everything NOW, but a clean home and organized life cannot be accomplished NOW. If you wanted to obtain a pilot's license, you could study and practice full-time for two weeks to a month and get one. That's not bad! But how many of us can dedicate an entire month to getting organized? The vast majority of us will need to be part-timers. A part-time student can get a pilot's license in four to six months' time. That is what you should expect with getting organized, too.

Our inner brats are going to look at that time frame and shriek that it isn't worth it! But we Wonder Women will get that first glorious taste of FLYing and will persevere for the long haul. We will persevere by remembering that not even baby birds can fly immediately; they remain in a messy nest for a while. Every fluttering baby step will bring us closer to the change we desire. Be patient, Wonder Sister!

EVENING ROUTINE

The Jewish day begins at sundown because God's description of a day begins with evening (Genesis 1:5). An organized day also begins in the evening.

Our old selves like to "wait until morning" to find the shoes, the clothes, and the papers we need for the day. The frustration and stress this approach produces are usually not enough to overcome our old selves' lazy fatigue. The old self tells herself she will get up early or just imagines she will have more energy the next day. She never does. We Wonder Women have to take control of the evenings.

The first step of FLYing is to establish an evening routine. The main purpose of this routine is to ensure a great start to our day. The result of a good evening routine is children who aren't looking for shoes, homework, or sports equipment in a panic. A Wonder Woman with an evening routine is not forced to choke down a breakfast bar while looking for her keys, only to discover the car is out of gas (not that I've ever experienced this).

My first evening routine consisted of shining my sink. Melanie used to do the dishes willy-nilly. The dishwasher was run all different times of day and usually she awoke to a sink full of dirty dishes. FLYLady's evening routine put an end to that. FLYLady said the kitchen was the heart of the home and the sink was the heart of the kitchen. A clean, shining sink would magically spread its clean glow to the rest of the kitchen.

I understood what she meant. I babysat as a Wonder Girl for a family whose uncluttered kitchen inspired me to clean. I think I inadvertently offended the mother, who would clean her house even more scrupulously each time I sat for the children, sure I thought her a poor housekeeper. On the contrary, the clean sink empty of dishes, the empty table, and the uncluttered floor gave me a passion for cleaning. If the dishes are done and the sink is clean, the whole kitchen feels clean. The magic that happens is you have an insatiable desire to carry the clean over to the rest of the kitchen.

FLYLady and friends talk about using cleanser on the sink and drying it out until it shines. The Perfection enemy often attacks at this point, telling you that you must dry the sink after each use. If you have no children at home and you aren't going to become the sink Nazi, do it if it makes you happy. I don't. I had a friend ask if it was okay to leave rinsed dishes out after a late night party since the dishwasher was full. I believe it is! The benefit of "shining your sink" is knowing the dishes are done. A further benefit for me is being able to assign unloading-the-dishwasher as a children's morning chore.

Once I'd established the clean-sink-at-bedtime habit, I added another step to my evening routine. I checked the calendar and weather. The information I got was useful in completing the next two steps. Melanie's calendar lives in her head. She neither writes down information on paper nor refers to the info after the fact. Wonder Women use a paper calendar.

My first calendar once I started FLYing was the More Time Moms calendar. I still use it. It hangs near my computer in the kitchen and has large squares for keeping track of all our family's information. I can write phone numbers and even directions to events in the squares and I keep invitations and sports schedules in the back pocket.

Calendars are very personal. There isn't any one calendar that is right for everyone. I've tried just about every kind: PDA, pocket, and DayTimer. Melanie's bad habits made them all useless. Wonder Women, however, can benefit from any of them. My current choice is the Memory Dock Creative Planner. It's perfect for scrapbookers, writers, and anyone with an artistic bent. The key to making any kind of calendar work is to keep it with us at all times. If you have no difficulties transferring information to your home calendar from notes or a secondary calendar, there is no need to change your system. But if you, like Melanie, lose your little slips of paper and never get around to copying information, you would do well to heed this advice.

I try to keep my Creative Planner with me at all times – even taking it with me from room to room. If I wake up in the morning with a great idea (or can't sleep until I write one down), I have a central place to put it. I use the Memory Dock Creative and Journal Docks to store old calendar pages, project notes, and writing for later retrieval. No longer do I allow Melanie to have five different notebooks going that I can't find. Only family events that my husband needs to be aware of are also listed on my More Time Moms calendar.

Once I've checked the calendar, I check the weather. I usually do this online so I don't have to wait for the newscasters to get around to sharing the information. When I know what the next day holds, I can plan my To Do list. My first approach to a To Do list was to list the top three goals I had for the next day on an index card. I kept the list to three so I wouldn't be overwhelmed or distracted by less important tasks. Now I often list more items in my planner, but star my top three. Wonder Women love the feeling of conquering all their To Do's in one day.

After writing my list of goals, I added preparing for the next day to my routine. Items that have to accompany me in the morning are put in the car or by the door and I defrost food for the next day's dinner if needed.

One of the most important ways I prepared for the next day as a new FLYer was to lay out clothes. At the time I began FLYing, I was a full-time stay-at-home mom. I wasn't wearing a Wonder Woman suit. I was wearing a frumpy suit – sweat pants, a t-shirt, slippers, and a pony tail. FLYLady filled my email's inbox with encouragement to dress in clothing that made me feel good about myself. Lay out some jewelry and wear it, she said. I understood the psychological effect of hair dos, clothes, and makeup. Once, Melanie went to high school without wearing makeup. Everyone commented that she looked ill. Before long, she began to feel awful!

Melanie was dressing like she was home for a sick day. No wonder she wasn't accomplishing anything. I began wearing clothes that told my brain I was going to work. My clothes were attractive but comfortable. I looked so nice people began to ask me where I was going. I felt I looked more appealing to my husband, too. The most important part of the outfit was the shoes. FLYLady recommended wearing shoes (not slippers) in the house so you could be ready to walk out the door at a moment's notice. Wearing shoes helped me take the charity donation to the car rather than put it off. I could also chase down a toddler who escaped the house. The shoes told Melanie she should be prepared to accomplish something. If you're adamantly against wearing shoes in the house, just make sure you find a way to let your inner brat know you're going to work for the day.

My closet is now organized and my laundry is caught up, so laying out a specific outfit isn't always necessary for me.

However, I usually lay out a specific outfit when preparing for church, a trip, or when I have to leave early in the morning.

Laying out clothes and shoes for children can also help create an orderly day. Children can help prepare for the next day as part of their evening routine at an early age. You can ask your children to choose an outfit, find shoes, and collect items needed for school or activities. I have also used weekly closet organizers to lay out children's clothing for the week. This preparation allows Dad to be of help in the mornings, too. No more "What should they wear?"

Once I had firmly established each of the preceding habits, I started taking care of my skin. Melanie was always too tired to take off her makeup at night. Disposable cleansing cloths made the task quick, giving me time to add moisturizer, too. Today I can't imagine not washing my face before bed, no matter how tired I am. You *can* create new habits!

My most recent habit is a quick after-dinner clean-up of the house and yard. Taking the time to pick up the toys, the dirty socks, and the newspapers will ensure the house you see upon awakening will make you smile.

The last step I added to my evening routine was keeping a regular bedtime. I will be honest and tell you my inner brat despises bedtime. I let her stay up late more often than I should. When that happens, I turn off my alarm in the morning, miss my prayer and Bible study time, and feel like I can't accomplish anything. Keeping the same sleep cycle is one of the most important things we can do for our health, energy, and organizational skills. If your brat keeps you up late, try to get up at the regular time anyway. You will be less tired if you do. Get your brat to bed by making sure she has free time during the day, giving her a bath, reading her a bedtime story, listening to quiet music, or saying prayers.

Melanie used to read books on getting organized that listed changes like the ones I've just described. She would immediately undertake all the changes at once. How does a child react to such drastic changes to her lifestyle? Yup. She rebels. If you want lasting change (and of course you do!), make one change at a time until you don't even have to think about it. Let it become part of what you do. You can also use the power of rewards to help you. For example, don't allow yourself to read a favorite book, listen to music, or take a relaxing shower or bath until your evening routine is done.

MORNING ROUTINE

A good evening routine is like the thrust required to get Wonder Woman's jet off the runway. The morning routine is just maintaining altitude. The most important part of the morning routine is *when* you arise. Waking up when the kids do, or worse yet, after the kids do, does not make for a productive day. When I am in charge of the day (and not Melanie), I get up an hour and a half before my kids do to pray, study, write, and shower/dress/put my shoes on.

My morning routine has always included prayer and Bible reading and/or study. Carol Barnier wrote *If I'm Diapering a Watermelon, Then Where'd I Leave the Baby?*. She advises us to use our morning habits (addictions) to help develop a prayer and study routine. Her coffee is her morning companion. I prefer orange juice. I often pour myself a glass prior to my quiet time. My other addiction is the Internet. I completed Beth Moore's *Living Beyond Yourself* Bible study by watching the videos online in the morning.[21] If you pair your favorite morning delight with the Bible and prayer, pretty soon you'll have developed a great practice.

I have tried many different approaches to my time with the Super Power – first thing in the morning or after showering, eating, or both. They all work for me. In the past, I have also exercised first thing in the morning. This is a good time for many Wonder Women to work out. You can easily combine exercise with prayer time. I enjoy listening to praise and worship music when I exercise, too.

My first morning routine included making the bed as soon as possible. I had spent a fortune on bed linens and fancy pillows that were usually lying in a heap on the floor. FLYLady suggests the bed is the heart of the bedroom like the sink is the heart of the kitchen. When the bed is made, the whole room feels clean. I have a lot of pillows, so it seemed like making the bed was more trouble than it was worth. I timed myself, however, and the whole process takes less than two minutes. That's not long to feel like the whole room is clean. My current routine includes making my bed while the children are doing their morning chores.

After I'd established the making-the-bed habit, I added cleaning the bathroom. Few enjoy cleaning bathrooms, but no one likes using a dirty one. The key to keeping it clean enough for company (and for you, too!) is to give it a quick wipe every day. I accomplish this by having cleaning wipes readily accessible. If you don't want to spend the money on wipes, you can keep your cleaning supplies out so all you have to do is squirt and wipe. You want to make the process as convenient as possible. Again, wiping out sinks and the toilet surface (I don't brush scrub every day) takes less than two minutes. I have more than one bathroom in my home and the kids have learned to do this quick wipe down in the other baths. The only thing I have to do for company is clean up after my distracted little boy and my toilet-paper-loving and towel-stealing toddler.

The last step in my morning routine is getting dinner started if I'm using the Crock-Pot. I love slow cooking because you can't help but have a good day if you know dinner's already done. And if you're home all day like I am, the smells are terrific! Crock-Pot cooking is even easier for me because I prepare meals in batches ahead of time using Saving Dinner's freezer meals.[22] Even if you're not using a slow cooker, you can gain a head start on your day by chopping veggies, for example. An even more basic step would be deciding what you're going to have. Then, if need be, you can stop by the store on your way home for any missing ingredients. When you're really FLYing, you will have a meal plan for the week and all your groceries on hand. For starters, however, thinking about what to make for dinner is good!

WEEKLY ROUTINE

You don't have to wait to begin a weekly routine until both your evening and morning routines are in place. A weekly routine is simply following God's example. He created each part of the world on a different day (Genesis 1-2). Melanie ran errands and did laundry whenever necessary. In the process, she was wasting time. My first weekly routine included one day of the week when I ran errands. I had a mother's helper that day. I knew to schedule doctor, dentist, and hair appointments for that day. I grocery shopped and often went on dates on that day as well. Don Aslett's book, *How to Handle 1,000 Things at Once*, taught me how to streamline my errands, saving time and money in the process.

My original weekly routine included a Home Blessing Hour on Mondays. This is the day the email reminder from FLYLady came out. FLYLady, with no young children at home, was able to vacuum (just the middles of the rooms), change linens, and clean tubs/showers in just one hour. My home is larger than FLYLady's and when I started, I had three children ages three and under. My Home Blessing Hour was more like two. FLYLady includes daily feather dusting of her entire house in her morning routine. The size of my house prohibits that, so I include dusting in my weekly routine. The feather duster does allow children to help and is effective on most surfaces – just not the ones the kids have wiped peanut butter and jelly on.

The way to minimize weekly cleaning chores ala FLYLady is to use a timer. Melanie would get distracted while cleaning or would become so perfectionistic that not much got done. The timer for each task allows it to be "good enough." Today the kids and I use a timer as well as music as a guide. We have also chosen to break up the weekly routine chores into daily chores we do in the evenings.

My original approach to doing laundry didn't work. I emptied all the hampers each morning, sorted, washed, and sorted again as I folded and put away. This approach left me feeling like the wash was never done. I finally decided to give my laundry a weekly routine, too. I chose to wash linens on Mondays (that's when we change them) and assigned everyone a day for their laundry. My older children are responsible for doing their own (see Chapter 12, "Working with Incredible Kids"). I leave laundry that isn't being done in the hampers and the only laundry I have to sort is my husband's, my own, and the younger children's.

FLYLady encourages us to make Saturday a family fun day and Sunday a day to renew the spirit. Doing short cleaning chores throughout the week enables us to spend less time cleaning during the weekend. We can spend our time doing what we and our families love to do. I try to avoid working on Sundays especially so I know I have one day each week to rest. After worshiping as a family, I can read, entertain friends or family, or spend time on hobbies.

Having basic routines was all I needed to be organized for many years. Today, because I homeschool six children, I rely on a more detailed schedule that incorporates my basic routines. *Managers of Their Homes* by Teri Maxwell taught me how to consider everything I wanted to do in a day and week, assign the amount of time each task required, and arrange a schedule for the children and me that incorporated it all. The magic of her system was thinking in terms of half-hours.

People always ask me how I have time to write and scrapbook and exercise. I have time because I assign time in the schedule. I write for thirty minutes in the morning and scrapbook and exercise for an hour respectively in the afternoon. Refining my schedule is an ongoing process. I've discovered, for example, that I won't get writing or scrapbooking done if I save these for evening. When I am done teaching for the day, I want a reward. Scrapbooking and reading while riding the bike at the gym fit the bill. If you protect the time, you will be amazed at what you can accomplish even if you only spare half an hour once a week. Mrs. Maxwell sews clothing for her family in just thirty minutes a day.

DECLUTTERING

Melanie had a housekeeper to clean. What she really needed help with was decluttering. No wonder she had trouble organizing. She had enough books, magazines, and papers to supply a library. Melanie was sure she would one day go through her three-year supply of *Woman's Day* magazines and clip the recipes she wanted for a book. There were mountains of clothes, toys, and memorabilia. She was sure the next child would need the clothes and toys and she couldn't part with the treasures of her past.

FLYLady's admonition to give or throw away items that weren't used, needed, or loved slowly allowed me to pry the clutter out of Melanie's desperate hands. The book *Find it in 5 Seconds* by Greg Vetter helped me come up with an orderly system for decluttering and filing papers. I have a small file box near my computer where I sort mail. Items go in the trash or in files such as "To Do Online," "Call," or "Mail."

I was able to convince Melanie the next baby wouldn't need six rattles to play with, but the impoverished babies served by Nurses for Newborns did.[23] I was also able to help Melanie keep a few clothing items that held the most memories and give away the rest. I went through each of the books I owned while on the phone and gave a friend the reason I was keeping them. When the reason was "I think I should read it because someone gave it to me" or "Someone might need this someday," my friend and I convinced Melanie she'd never make time to read the undesirable books and that she recommend titles rather than lending them.

When I started decluttering, the basement was a mess. I hated going down there. I called it the Dungeon. I made myself go down there every day and set the timer for five minutes. I was amazed to find my entire basement was in order in a matter of weeks, working just minutes a day. The key to decluttering is short work periods. The most important part of the time-limited strategy is FLYLady's recommendation that you not take out more than you can put away in an hour. Pulling out all the garage's contents the hour before it starts to rain isn't a good plan. Clean the garage one box or one shelf at a time.

Perfection will tell you you'll never get it done if you don't do it all at once. The truth is you'll never get it done if you don't do it one step at a time. Most of the decluttering I do takes no more than fifteen minutes a day. And remember this: The only way you'll ever have everything perfectly decluttered is when you're dead. An orderly home is one that is decluttered a little bit every day. When you *are* dead, your loved ones can walk down memory lane instead of wading through your clutter.

FLYING to NEW YORK

I had found the freedom in FLYing when I saw that *Woman's Day* magazine was looking for nominations of women who make a difference in their communities. I immediately thought of Sharon Rohrbach, founder of Nurses for Newborns, an organization that provides nursing care and baby supplies to at-risk and indigent babies. I put the magazine in my pile of To Dos and didn't get to it until a couple of months later (that must have been Melanie's fault).

I emailed a letter of recommendation saying a brief prayer that Sharon might win and forgot about it. A few months later, Sharon told me she was one of the finalists. I was stunned! I soon learned Sharon would be receiving her award from the First Lady in New York City. I was thrilled for her. I was even more delighted when the editor of *Woman's Day* magazine called and asked if I would like to meet First Lady, Laura Bush, too!

The opportunity to meet with editors of a magazine with a 6,000,000 circulation was a tremendous one for a writer like me. I knew I needed to have an article idea ready to pitch to them. I was at the gym one day praying about what my idea should be when FLYLady came to mind. I thought, "Yes, that would be perfect, but she hasn't responded to my email." I'd recorded a "Woman to Woman" radio broadcast with Phyllis Wallace and had sent FLYLady a link to it online. I'd never heard anything.

When I came home and checked my email that day, FLYLady had responded! The email had gotten lost. She consented to being interviewed for an article, I was able to convince an editor to do the story, and a woman who was once living with roaches became a Wonder Woman writing about organization for *Woman's Day*.

IT'S ALL ABOUT THE LOVE

When we're really FLYing, we can easily look down on those who aren't. We can become demanding and harsh. Melanie takes control and goes on a Martha Stewart ego trip. She barks at Superman for not putting things in the proper place in the freezer. She yells at the kids for not picking up the playroom while she is chatting online. When we stop loving, we stop FLYing.

Reportedly, one of Lynda Carter's favorite songs is Irving Berlin's "Always." I like to imagine the Super Power singing it to us as we clean and organize:

I'll be loving you always
With a love that's true always.
When the things you've planned
Need a helping hand,
I will understand always.

Always.

Days may not be fair always,
That's when I'll be there always.
Not for just an hour,

Not for just a day,
Not for just a year,
But always.

We may not always have our To Do list done, our beds made, or dinner in the Crock-Pot, but if we have love, we will never fail (1 Corinthians 13:8).

With Justice for All

The League is my family, Superman. I'll do what I must to protect it. That is the only promise I can give. Take it or leave it.
Wonder Woman, *Justice League*

Lynda Carter's Wonder Woman worked alone. But comics and animated cartoons tell us of Wonder Woman's strong alliance with other great superheroes: Superman, Batman, Flash, Green Lantern, Aquaman, and many others, including female characters like Hawkwoman. Wonder Woman lends her power to, and receives help from, the Justice League.

We Wonder Women are most powerful when we have a cast of supporting superheroes. We need the help of our Wonder Sisters and an entire league of those filled with the Super Power. Our Super Friends keep us humble, provide practical help and assistance, and encourage us to grow in Super Power.

Thomas Higginson said great [wo]men "are rarely isolated mountain peaks; they are summits of ranges." I talk with many women who want to live alone, majestically, with their heads in the clouds. They are confident they alone can draw upon the Super Power and solve their own problems. But we were not created to live alone.

When the Super Power created the first Wonder Woman, it was with the express purpose that man not be alone (Genesis 2:18). In Ecclesiastes 4:9-10, the Super Power tells us:

> Two are better than one, because they have a good return for their work: If one falls down, his friend can help him up. But pity the man who falls and has no one to help him up!

In the movie, *Spiderman 3*, Spiderman's girlfriend reminds him, "Everybody needs help – even Spiderman." Even Wonder Woman needs the help of friends to change.

JUSTICE LEAGUE HEADQUARTERS

One of the headquarters mentioned in the Justice League comics is the Secret Sanctuary. If we want to be part of the League of Superfriends, this is where we must gather. It is where we learn of the enemy's latest work and are instructed how to defeat him. The Sanctuary is also where we worship the Super Power and are renewed in our faith.

Sadly, many Wonder Sisters don't believe in "organized religion." Some have had bad experiences in church. I've spoken to women who've been deeply hurt by pastors, church leaders, and other professing Christians. I've heard people say the church is full of hypocrites. A pastor once joked that when someone makes this statement he replies, "No it isn't. There's room for you, too!"

The church is a sanctuary for Wonder Women and Supermen, but every superhero hauls their old self into the building. The crowding that ensues makes for some conflict. Even the comic book Wonder Woman had some trouble with the members of the Justice League. Bruce Timm, creator of Wonder Woman's character for "Justice League," explains:

> ...[Her voice] is not haughty or imperious, but she is a Princess and is used to being treated with a certain amount of deference. She doesn't quite get that from the League, so Wonder Woman is a little taken aback by that. It makes for interesting conflicts. [24]

TAKEN ABACK

Years ago, I spoke to a group of caregivers at my church on the topic, "Coping with Challenging Christians." I based my talk largely on the book, *How to Get Along with Difficult People* by Florence Littauer. I had a great time presenting Florence's light-hearted material, using funny names to describe those who annoy us.

Although I could tell my audience enjoyed my jokes, I noted their careful attention to my words. When I was finished speaking, a woman said, "That was a lot of material. Can we get that in writing?" I was happy to comply and happy also to give specific counsel when this same woman asked for it. I felt like I had the answers to give. After all, I was Wonder Woman with a Ph.D.

Sure, Melanie once had a heap of people problems living in the roach motel, but she'd moved far away from her troublesome neighbors. At the time of my presentation, I was working for a Christian counseling agency, helping the people that drove others crazy. I felt fortunate I only had to deal with the same difficult people once a week. My work gave me a sense of control over challenging people and my personal life didn't include them. I had a new group of friends at my church and in my women's Bible study. Problem people were relegated to Melanie's past – or so I thought.

I was so excited to be part of the Justice League. I met all kinds of different superheroes. I was eager to work for good and combat evil alongside them. In our Sanctuary, I learned more about the Super Power and His plan for my life. I spent time with people who were more than friends; they were my family. Hebrews 2:11 tells us that the Super Power and those who receive His power are part of the same family. I never dreamt that my most powerful adversaries would be those in my own family, but they were.

I was shocked when I saw a mean-spirited staff member attack another in the Christian counseling agency I worked for. Melanie had seen her share of that in graduate school, but I never expected to see it in those with the Super Power. This was a mild skirmish. Soon I would see an all-out war in a place I least expected it: my Sanctuary.

I saw the people I loved, my fellow superheroes, allow their old selves to run amok in the church. Their gossip, slander, and rejection were like kryptonite that crippled the

League's leaders. Meanwhile, the infighting allowed the enemy to gain ground.

Like Wonder Woman who sees a foe wound her Super Friends, I was greatly distressed and wanted to lead the rescue effort. But the enemy called in reinforcements and those I once called friends bound me in my own lasso and I was rendered powerless.

The Wonder Woman of comics had a long-time friend who was brainwashed into hating the heroine and sought to destroy her. The ex-friend, the Silver Swan, joined Villainy, Inc., an all-female group of super villains whose primary goal was to destroy Wonder Woman.

I lived that story line. I couldn't believe people I had loved so deeply could betray me the way they did. I drew near to the Super Power and He slowly freed me from the bondage of my affliction. I consoled myself with the idea it had been a fluke. There had been miscommunication. I had made some mistakes. I had joined forces with the wrong friends. I knew it couldn't happen again. But it did. Over and over again.

I began to doubt my identity as Wonder Woman. The superheroes I'd called friends said I wasn't. Maybe I wasn't? Maybe I had a dark side I couldn't see, but others could. I lived in fear that I would join forces with more Wonder Sisters who would turn out to be Silver Swans who hated me. And worst of all, I feared it would be my fault.

I sought the counsel of a psychologist friend who wondered how I attracted such crazies. Her assurance of my normality didn't help. I didn't want to be normal. I was Wonder Woman. I believed with the Super Power, I should be able to make the Justice League work. I prayed. I forgave. I was kind. But my friends continued to fall away and my list of opponents grew.

I can identify with the Wonder Woman of comics who can never rest as she deals with growing numbers of people who despise her. She wants to serve others with the Super Power given to her, but it seems to infuriate, rather than thrill.

QUIT FOOL-ING AROUND

I was really feeling defeated when I sought the counsel of another Wonder Sister. She, too, had battle scars from Super Friends who'd attacked her. She gave me a book that brought rest to my weary soul: *Fool-Proofing Your Life* by Jan Silvious.

Jan described a different category of difficult person than I had discussed in my presentation at church. This kind of person wasn't just annoying and I didn't find them amusing. This kind is not open to change. In fact, nothing we do as Wonder Women will change them. We won't see change when we say we're sorry, apologize, kiss up to them, avoid the hot topics, give them reading material, or encourage counseling. Only the Super Power can change them.

Our mission on earth is to love the Super Power and to love others. Our mission is not to change people. That's the Super Power's job. I knew that. Even in my work as a Christian psychologist, I understood I wasn't changing anyone. God must work change in others, just as He did in me.

Yet somehow I took "Turn the other cheek" and "Give to him who asks" as a commandment to endure continuing abuse. I wasn't giving equal weight to other Bible passages. 1 Samuel 19 tells of David, "a man after God's own heart" fleeing his former friend, Saul, whose jealousy incited him to murderous rage. Even Jesus walked away from mistreatment that didn't serve a higher purpose (John 8:59).

Jan describes a person that the Bible terms a Fool. Fools are obviously those who do foolish things, but a true Fool is typically:

✓ Closed-minded and always right
✓ Spiritually lost and hardened, even if religious
✓ Complacent and happy with her foolishness
✓ Deceitful as in two-faced and slanderous
✓ Angry and destructive to peace and relationships
✓ Wearisome

As I read this description, I found myself both relieved and heartbroken. I was relieved I wasn't crazy. I was relieved it wasn't my fault. I was relieved there was nothing I was supposed to be doing to solve the problem. But I was heartbroken that people I loved couldn't be part of my Justice League.

Oh I could love my Fools, Jan told me. I couldn't help but love them! I could see them, relate to them, and be kind to them, Jan said. But they couldn't serve with me in the Justice League, my trusted inner circle. I grieved for them and for what they could be. I wished there were something I could do to restore the relationships besides pray.

As much as I found peace in *Fool-Proofing Your Life*, something bothered me. I felt sorry for my Fools. The author had differentiated between a genuine Fool and someone who occasionally does foolish things. I understood the difference. I saw that I wasn't a Fool because I didn't live consistently as one, but some of those I loved *were* bona fide Fools. Then I remembered my old roommate.

Remember her? Your old self? The woman we've called Flesh Woman and your inner brat? What I realized is she's a Fool, too. It isn't just that we Wonder Women occasionally do foolish things; we all have a Fool living inside us. That's why I have such sympathy for my Fools. But our inner Fool is also the reason we can't let our Fool-ish friends and family members get too close. Proverbs 13:20 says, "He who walks with the wise grows wise, but a companion of fools suffers harm."

When our inner Fool gets together with other Fools, there's gonna be some harm done. I still hurt because of that harm and I bet you could tell me some stories, too! So how on earth are we supposed to be in a league with our Wonder Sisters when we know we could easily deteriorate into a bunch of Fools? And what if our Fools are part of our family?

Jan doesn't recommend divorce or termination of relationship except where the Bible clearly makes provision for it. What she does recommend is thinking of ourselves as a castle. When our Fools want to gain access to the most vulnerable part of us (especially the room where our inner Fool lives), we draw up the drawbridge. We keep our Fools at an emotional distance. Pulling up that drawbridge by ourselves is too heavy a task. We're Wonder Women, but we're going to need the Super Power for this one.

We have to pray for wisdom and ask the Super Power to show us how to love our Fools without letting our guard down. We must also continue to pray the Lord would bring those we love to faith in Jesus. Jesus knows what it is to love a Fool who betrays. His close friend, Judas, sold him out for money. Even when Judas was confronted with his unfaithfulness, he did not repent (Matthew 26). We can be comforted in knowing we have a Savior familiar with our suffering (Isaiah 53:3).

The Justice League of comics and television frequently lost and gained many members. We Wonder Women have to be open to an ever-changing Justice League roster, too – painful as it may be. The changes we desire in our lives as Wonder Women may only come when we join forces with a new Wonder Sister. I have found a true blue friend is the best encouragement for letting go of a Fool.

HOW DO YOU FIND HER?

In fantasy land, heroes appear out of thin air. In real life, a good friend can be hard to find. School and work provide ample opportunities for making friends, but when you've moved, changed careers, decided to stay home, or had a bad experience with friends, building a new support group can be tough.

Wonder Sisters can usually be found a-plenty in the Sanctuary. Sitting through a Sunday service and leaving won't be enough, however. I didn't make friends at church until I

started volunteering and participating in small groups. If you
don't belong to a church, find one that not only believes the
Bible is the Word of God, but also welcomes you and helps
you join a small group. Larger churches with a small group
ministry have a variety of groups that build relationships –
groups that focus on Bible study, service, fellowship or
specific needs or interests.

A second place to find friends is through your child's
school. Asking about homework assignments, getting
involved in the classroom or the PTA, and offering to
carpool are all good ways to open the door to a possible
friendship. I met my closest girlfriends at my children's
sports practices and games.

A third place to build relationships is online. Years ago I
believed looking for friends on the Internet was like
hitchhiking: It was for weirdos who weren't afraid of getting
hurt! I was wrong. By posting messages on an electronic
bulletin board (using a nickname), I met some wonderful
ladies with families like mine. We eventually continued our
friendship with an email group. As we built trust, we began
sharing Christmas cards, gifts, and phone calls. Some of us
have met in person and felt as comfortable as if we were
"real life" friends. To find friends online, post on a message
board (try www.christianforums.com) or join an email group
(try www.yahoogroups.com) with shared interests or
circumstances.

A fourth place to connect with women is in your
neighborhood. Going for a walk and getting out in the yard
to garden or play with the kids is an easy way to meet other
active women. I met most of my neighbors through informal

get-togethers. I've attended block parties at my neighbors' homes and I've invited ladies to my home once a month for dessert and a fun theme-related activity.[25]

Finally, you can find a gal pal by taking a class or joining a hobby group. I took a beginners' tennis class through adult continuing education and met women who enjoyed playing the sport as much as I did. Some of the women who joined me in a weight loss class more than ten years ago are still some of my closest friends.

I have taken risks in going to classes and conferences alone. I have put myself out there when it was hard. I've been hurt and disappointed and lonely at times, but the fun and the love and the prayers have been worth it. Is there a way to reduce the risk in our quest for female companionship? I think so. We can determine if she's a friend or foe early in the acquaintanceship.

IS SHE RIGHT FOR YOU?

There are many articles and books on how to find the right man, but very little help in identifying a good friend. We can keep an acquaintance that doesn't pass this test, but a Wonder Sister allowed to join the League, our inner circle, should be:

✓ A wise woman (Proverbs 3:35)
✓ A respected woman (Proverbs 11:16)
✓ Willing to learn (Proverbs 12:15)
✓ Willing to work hard (Proverbs 6:6)
✓ Reading and studying God's Word (Psalm 19:7).

✓ Kind and truthful (Psalm 36:3)

✓ Slow to anger (Proverbs 22:24)

✓ Striving for obedience to God (Psalm 107:43)

✓ Friends with other superheroes (1 Corinthians 15:30)

✓ Encouraging (Romans 15:2)

✓ Helpful when trouble comes (Proverbs 17:17)

✓ Willing to confront you if necessary (Proverbs 27:6)

✓ Sincere in giving advice (Proverbs 27:9)

✓ Willing to rejoice with you (Song of Solomon 1:4)

✓ Willing to mourn with you (Job 2:11)

Checklist or no checklist, the Holy Spirit will warn us if a relationship is not right. Beth Moore calls this being "Six Flags over Texas."[21] I've been "Six Flags" many times and ignored the signs, probably because I wasn't spending enough time listening to God and studying the Bible. I was also under the assumption I had to be friends with anyone who chose me, especially if the chooser was a professing Christian. I now understand Melanie likes to hold on to relationships like she does her clutter. Even if she no longer loves a friendship, she thinks she should keep it around because she might need it someday. Ask God and not your inner brat for wisdom in choosing your league of friends.

A TRUE FRIEND

I once counseled a young woman whose standards for her friends were impossibly high. She thought they should call the night before each of her college exams to encourage her and should follow up the next day to see how she did.

Her friends weren't allowed to have lives of their own. This young lady thought all her problems could be corrected if her friends would only be more thoughtful. I have a feeling her friends wanted to give her a thought full alright!

Often without realizing it, we let the Fool inside us demand more from our girlfriends than is reasonable or fair, even going as far as expecting our friends to run our race for us. We can unwittingly make our walking partner, diet buddy, or sponsor our god. When they fail us, we have an excuse for our failure to change. Yet every friend, family member, and pastor we have will eventually fail us – except Jesus.

One of my favorite hymns is "What a Friend We Have in Jesus." Jesus is a friend who is always there when we need Him. He's a friend who'll always tell us the truth in love. He's a friend who'll challenge us to be our best because He *is* the best. Although it's inappropriate to ask a friend to exercise for us, do our jobs for us, or parent our children for us, Jesus wants to be asked to do it all through us. A girlfriend who did everything for us would get burned out and leave us. Not Jesus. He can't get burned out because He's all-powerful and He's promised never to betray us. If we had no other friends, Jesus would be friend enough.

If we want to call Him friend, He says we must love one another (John 13:35). Loving means befriending. As much as you may long for a friend who will fight for change alongside you, recognize that others share your longing. Some of the loneliest people appear to be the most popular. If you want a good friend, be one. Listen to God's prompting and introduce yourself to others. Be willing to be more and more vulnerable with fellow Wonder Women. You'll be amazed by what God's Super Power can do when two or more of His daughters join forces. No fooling.

Winning with Superman

I'm not a prophet or a stone aged man, just a mortal with potential of a Superman. I'm living on.
David Bowie

elanie met Clark Kent 15 years ago. He wasn't wearing a stuffy business suit with his black glasses; he had his own brand of not-cool. He wore a loud tropical shirt that was buttoned too low. The only thing missing was the gold necklace. He danced enthusiastically, but poorly. His opening line was, "Can I have your phone number?" Not exactly the beginning of a fairy tale romance, unless we're talking "Frog Prince."

Melanie told him she'd say her phone number one time and if he remembered it, fine. She figured the only number that would register in his brain later was the number of beers he'd consumed. She was surprised when he called the next evening. They arranged a date at the same bar they'd met in.

The date didn't do much to convince Melanie that a kiss would remove the many warts she saw. He showed her a stack of pictures of his recent trip. Nearly every picture had him showing off his physique in a muscle shirt. In case she didn't notice how fit he was, there were pictures of him lifting huge boulders. Melanie couldn't recall Superman ever showing off for Lois Lane.

Melanie didn't know why she agreed to another date. Maybe she was surprised the guy didn't try to hide his faults like all the others. It wasn't long before she grew weary of the faults, however. He insisted they meet at the same bar for each date. There was no dinner and sometimes no conversation either. He often left her at the table while he visited with his friends.

Melanie reasoned that Susan Deitz had been right. Her book, *Single File: How to Live Happily Forever After With Or Without Prince Charming,* convinced her she didn't need to wait for a prince to start living like a queen. Getting married was an obsession keeping her from ending bad relationships and becoming the woman she wanted to be. Per Ms. Deitz's advice, she imagined she would never marry and started making choices accordingly. The first decision she made was Clark had to go.

She was pretty surprised when he took the break-up so well. He agreed he had some warts that needed to be removed and he understood why Melanie was unhappy. So she gave him another chance. After all, Clark Kent may not knock your socks off, but he's a pretty likable guy.

Unfortunately for Melanie, the frog stayed a frog and Melanie was ready to kiss him good-bye once again. She dumped Clark for a big strong football player, hopeful she'd found her prince. The new guy's habit of constantly complimenting her was encouraging. Melanie asked him to be her date for her cousin's wedding. During the ceremony, the soon-to-be-married couple had difficulty lighting the unity candle so everyone laughed. The soloist, a family friend, thought everyone was laughing at him. He was so nervous, he forgot the words and began stammering. Melanie's boyfriend, who sat head and shoulders above everyone in the church, boomed out, "Man! This guy can't sing! He's terrible!"

After Melanie chastised Football Boy for his lack of social skills, she felt the Spirit of God say, "You're going to marry Clark." So strongly was this statement impressed upon her, she told her mother she would soon be Mrs. Clark Kent. It wasn't that Clark seemed much less the ogre now that she'd really been with one. It was more like she was Fiona and Clark was Shrek. Melanie realized she was a princess who was also an ogre. That insight helped her see Clark differently. Suddenly he looked a lot like Superman!

Once she saw the Superman in Clark, she made the mistake of thinking Clark was history. He wasn't. His goofy self showed up when she least expected him. The biggest problem was Melanie loved fighting with Clark. Whenever Clark came out to play, so did that brat Melanie. In their first year of marriage, friends called the couple the Bickersons. They fought about almost everything. When Superman and I took over, we couldn't believe how childish those two were. Sometimes we'd laugh about their antics, but other times we feared they would destroy our marriage. We determined we needed the Super Power to hold on to the love we had for each other.

WHY DOES HE DO THAT?

I knew Clark wasn't Superman, but I couldn't figure out why he did things the way he did. Why did he try to tell me how to make pancakes? Why did he get angry at inanimate objects? Why did he care what I bought?

The only husband I had experience with was my dad. Clark was nothing like him. My dad used to sit in the middle of the mall eating ice cream while Mom and I shopped. He would pretend to be interested when we showed him our purchases. Clark, on the other hand, insisted on choosing the china we put on our wedding registry. Clark enjoyed haggling for the best price on furniture and tried on more clothes and shoes than I did.

I assumed Clark was just trying to irritate me. He was certainly succeeding! And he *really* got under Melanie's skin. She enjoyed shopping and cooking and expected Clark to get out of her way!

Florence and Marita Littauer gave me insight into the Clark problem during a CLASS speakers conference.[26] The two women explained the influence of personality type on relationships. I had studied personality assessment in graduate school, but didn't remember much about it. People who knew I was a psychologist would say, "I'm an EFNP. What are you?" IDK! I could never remember what the letters stood for. The Littauers described four basic types that were easy for me to remember:

> **Sanguine**. This personality wants to have fun. He's talkative, popular, and enjoys being the center of attention. He can be childish, irresponsible, disorganized, and loud.

Choleric. This personality wants control. He's hard-driving, ambitious, and a natural leader. When he feels out-of-control, he can be angry and unsympathetic.

Melancholy. This personality wants perfection. He's detail-oriented, organized, sensitive, and often musically talented. Because perfection isn't possible, he's often depressed and unwilling to give compliments.

Phlegmatic. This personality wants peace. He's likable, balanced, relaxed, and satisfied with his lot in life. Because he fears conflict, he may be uncommunicative and indecisive.[27]

I quickly determined Clark was a Choleric/Sanguine and I was a Sanguine/Choleric.

The personalities explained Clark's and Melanie's bad behaviors. Clark became difficult when he wasn't in control. He wanted to be part of the decision-making process even when it came to shopping. He became frustrated when he couldn't get something to work. Melanie quit cleaning and organizing when it stopped being fun. She was unhappy in her marriage when she wasn't getting positive attention. Because both Melanie and Clark wanted control, conflict was inevitable.

But personality also explained why the marriage worked. I loved having a Superman who was a productive leader. He loved having a fun Wonder Woman who was also achievement-oriented.

Even though learning the personalities assured me Clark wasn't trying to annoy me, I was still disappointed every time I saw him. I wanted a full-time Superman. I tried to get rid of Clark for good. It seemed like I'd have success for a day, then back would come the old Clark.

Whatever his personality, Melanie didn't like the way Clark handled his emotions, parented the kids, spent his time, expressed himself romantically, or spent his money. Although she'd failed to fix herself, she figured she could fix Clark. When Clark was handled, she thought changing herself would be easy.

To have her full-time Superman, she tried reasoning with Clark. It didn't work. She tried rewarding Clark. It didn't work. She tried rebuking Clark. It didn't work. After much effort and many tears, she finally gave up trying and I was able to step in.

SURRENDER

I realized wisdom was required. I read *The Surrendered Wife* by Laura Doyle. The book suggests husbands need to lead in their marriages in order to be Supermen. The problem, according to Mrs. Doyle, is that women often overpower their husbands without realizing it. If we allow them to lead, she said, we'll find they're the Superman we want them to be. If we don't, we'll have to put up with Clark Kent. One suggestion Mrs. Doyle made was to say "Whatever you think" when our husbands are making a decision. This response was supposed to encourage a man to assume leadership as well as responsibility.

I had the opportunity to practice this technique when Clark told me he hoped to attend a baseball game that evening. Melanie went nuts when she heard that. She reminded me Clark had been out two nights that week already and she needed help with the kids so she could complete an important project. With great effort, I ignored Melanie and said, "Whatever you think."

Astonished, Clark said, "Whatever I think? Whatever I think? Okay, I'm going." I bit my tongue so Melanie couldn't say anything. Her whining and pouting made me miserable while he was gone. But when Clark came home, he put on his Superman suit and said, "I wish I hadn't gone to the game. The whole time I felt guilty knowing you needed my help." Hm. That got me thinking. I decided to pursue more wisdom for winning with my Superman.

I read *On the Other Side of the Garden* by Virginia Fugate and discovered the Super Power wanted me to trust Him to work through my imperfect husband. The Bible tells of Sarah who lied as directed by her husband, Abraham. Because Abraham was afraid he would be killed on account of his beautiful wife, he asked Sarah to say she was only his sister. She was nearly taken in marriage by the Pharaoh until God intervened (Genesis 12). Abraham nearly lost his wife once, but chose to lie about Sarah again, putting her in the same dangerous situation (Genesis 20). Melanie never would have allowed her husband to make the same mistake twice! And she never would have experienced God's power and protection the way Sarah did.

Created to Be His Helpmeet by Debi Pearl challenged me to rethink my role as wife. She wrote about God's plan for marriage. I was created to help Clark be Superman, she told me. Clark wasn't created to help me be Wonder Woman. It took me a long time to finish Mrs. Pearl's book. Each page felt like a dagger in Melanie's heart. I was shocked when I realized the marriage difficulties we had weren't all Clark's fault. Melanie and her spiritual arrogance were also to blame.

Even though I'd had to shut Melanie up about the Bible's boring irrelevance in order to get it read, once she finished it, Melanie was quite proud of her newfound knowledge. She rarely missed an opportunity to let Clark know who wore the smarty pants in the family. I needed to shut her up again.

I decided, based on the Bible's teachings on marriage, to give Superman the opportunity to be the spiritual leader of the family. I'd always wanted Clark to lead family devotions – fun activities that teach biblical truth. Melanie thought it was hopeless. She knew Clark didn't care about those books and she couldn't picture him gathering up supplies for the lesson. Then I realized if I was created to help Clark, I could easily do those things for him. I figured all I had to do was confirm a time, collect the materials, and give Clark the book to read. To my delight, Clark agreed to lead. I had high hopes that Superman would soon be making his appearance.

He did. The first time Superman led this family time, I was very excited – so excited I let Melanie get the best of me. When Superman shared half the lesson, she jumped in and explained what it all meant. He said, "That's just what I was going to say." I was shocked at how controlling Melanie could be and became more determined than ever to keep her quiet. I loved seeing Superman in charge and I was willing to do what it took to see him more often. First, I had to do battle with another enemy.

QUEEN CLEA

Wonder Woman doesn't try to control Superman, but Queen Clea does. She rules Venturia where women dominate men. This cruel leader is one of the comic-book enemies we haven't discussed. Her desire for control of men is the fallout from the first Wonder Woman's disobedience (Genesis 3:16). We can inadvertently follow Queen Clea's lead by believing women's liberation means lording over men. Wonder Women are strong women entitled to justice, but not to rule their husbands (Colossians 3:18). God gave men authority in marriage and also responsibility for it.

Bible teacher, David Jeremiah, told of his early years in marriage and ministry on his radio program "Turning Point." He said he was gone all day and evening building his church and neglected his wife and young children at home. At dinner one evening, David's wife asked him if he planned on working again that night. He said of course he was! She said she wasn't going to nag him about his neglect of his family because she knew he was accountable to God for his church *and* his family. David shared that no amount of complaining or controlling would have had a greater impact on him than those words. Our husbands answer to a higher authority, even if they don't recognize Him.

I hated to admit it, but Queen Clea's influence was wreaking havoc on my marriage. The Queen saw Clark as the enemy and so did I. While we fought, our real enemies were gaining on us. I finally understood (after taking a few beatings) that to be victorious in the battle for change, I needed Superman by my side. My mission from the Super Power wasn't to make Clark Superman; it was to make sure I was Wonder Woman.

SUPERMAN M.I.A.

I can understand why Superman doesn't show for Melanie. But when I'm Wonder Woman and he's a no-show, I'm really let down. Many of my Wonder Sisters experience the same disappointment. After doing everything right, they're still stuck with Mr. Wrong. Their Clark spends all of his time working or on the couch. Their Clark wants sex on his own terms or not at all. Their Clark spends carelessly or controls it all. Their Clark drinks, smokes, swears, yells, lies, or even cheats. Worst of all, their Clark doesn't believe in a Super Power. Some of my Wonder Sisters complain they're not sure they've ever even *seen* him as Superman. The temptation to look for a hero elsewhere is great. What can we do to stay true while we wait for Superman to appear?

Promise. You made a promise of faithfulness to God and your husband. Remind your husband of your commitment. He may be testing it. Wonder Women keep their promise until the marriage ends – even during a separation.

Prioritize. Superman doesn't show when we're looking up to someone else. If our allegiance to children, parents, friends, work, hobbies, or even church supersedes our allegiance to him, we may see a bird or a plane, but we won't see Superman. In *Superman Returns*, Lois Lane breaks Superman's heart by writing "Why the World Doesn't Need Superman." Don't break your hero's heart. Show him you need him.

Praise. Superman loves appreciation and respect. If we don't give it to him, he'll find someone who will. If his behavior doesn't seem praiseworthy, remember Melanie's rat. Praise behavior that is anywhere close to what you want and ignore behaviors that aren't. Who says you can't teach an old rat new tricks?

Prepare. Superman won't appear just anywhere. The circumstances have to be right. He'll arrive in the midst of crowds and chaos, but if we want him to ourselves, we may want to clean the house, cook a meal, and put the kids to bed early.

Preach. We can remind ourselves of the value of our Supermen and of marriage when we encourage other women. Every year when I counsel engaged couples, I find I am sustained in my own marriage.

Practice. We have to be Wonder Women if we expect our men to be Supermen. A true heroine is one who does the right thing even when it's hard. A marriage to Mr. Wrong doesn't make your bad behavior right.

Preserve. Superman's good deeds are always recorded in the newspaper. We can record the good times with Superman, too. Review photos of happy memories with your husband often so you aren't tempted to give him bad press. A scrapbook I made of my love and respect for my husband is one of his most treasured possessions.

Pray. Because our husbands are under God's authority, we have to go over their heads when they're not showing up for work. Daily prayer for our husbands releases God's power to change us and them. Romans 5:3-5 reassures us that persevering prayer is never a waste of time: "Not only so, but we also rejoice in our sufferings, because we know that suffering produces perseverance; perseverance, character; and character, hope. And hope does not disappoint us, because God has poured out his love into our hearts by the Holy Spirit, whom he has given us."

Your Clark may require another approach. Seek God and wise counsel and consider other options such as medical testing, marriage mentoring, a Christian marriage retreat, counseling, intervention, rehab, a domestic violence shelter, or separation.

OUR GROOM

One day the Super Power gave me a vision. It was like seeing my wedding on video. I was walking down the aisle in my gown to a handsome Groom in white. He was every bit as handsome as a romance cover guy. His eyes radiated love for me like I had never known. I wanted to be wrapped in His arms forever. I knew He would never hurt or betray me and marriage to Him would exceed my greatest expectations.

But as I neared the altar, He looked to my right. So did I. There was Clark in the same black tux I'd married him in. He looked nice and happy to see me, but I knew he would hurt me. I knew he would disappoint me. I wanted the Groom in white, but when I looked at Him longingly, He told me with His eyes to marry Clark. Clark would become more of the man I needed him to be, He said. I didn't need to worry, He told me, because He would be right there with me as my forever Groom.

I know it sounds like a bizarre twist on the movie, *Ghost*, but I got the message. We are all married to Clark who is sometimes Superman. When Superman disappears, we can still spend time with the Super Power. When Clark is angry, we can be with the Prince of Peace. When Clark is selfish, we can enjoy the Giver of all things. When Clark doesn't love us, we can spend time with the Lover of our souls.

Superman may not return to us, but Jesus will. Our Hero has rescued us from death and has the power to save our marriage. Call on Him.

Working with Incredible Kids

Your identity is your most valuable possession. Protect it.
Helen to her children, *The Incredibles*

After nearly ten months of pregnancy and thirty hours of labor, a creature emerged from my body that was both familiar and foreign. He had some of me and some of his dad and he was something else – a seven pound, seven ounce wonder! I really liked the guy who gave me the epidural, but I was crazy about my baby boy.

At first our Incredible baby seemed to have inherited none of Clark's or Melanie's characteristics. Superman and I were both relieved and proud of our little guy's superior growth during his first year. By age two, however, his super strength of will became a cause for concern.

I decided to begin training my young superhero so he could use the potty. Because I had such an exceptional child, I chose the fast track to potty training. I bought a book on toilet training in a day. The author had successfully trained developmentally disabled children in a day with the method he espoused so I was sure I could train my Incredible boy in no time at all.

The one-day method appealed to the psychologist in me. I was to keep my son and his potty chair in the kitchen. I was also to give him dry salty snacks and plenty to drink. It seemed a lot like putting a rat in a cage – something I knew how to do. When my boy peed in his potty I was to praise him. When he had an accident, I was to run my son back and forth to the potty ten times to practice the right behavior. By the end of the day, the author assured me, I would have a toilet-trained child.

My Super boy loved the snacks and drinks, but didn't like the potty chair. He refused to sit on it and when I encouraged him to run to the potty after an accident, he had a temper tantrum. Rats! That was the day I knew he had some Clark in him. Things really got messy when Melanie joined the potty party. She was furious when little Clark wouldn't cooperate. The Ph.D. in psychology was humiliated that she couldn't toilet train a normal child in a day when the author could train disabled children in no time at all.

Melanie wasn't about to give up control of the situation. She asked other moms for advice. She bought several special potty chairs. She made potty prize charts. She read a pediatrician's article. She wrapped surprise gifts to be opened for each potty success. When nothing motivated little Clark, she asked him, "What prize would you like for going potty?" He said, "Nothing. I don't wanna go potty."

Little Clark wanted nothing to do with the potty when he was two and a half. He wanted nothing to do with the potty when he was three. And he wanted nothing to do with the potty when he was three and a half. Melanie was tired of changing diapers, but she was sick to death of trying to change her son. She finally quit and I took over the training.

TRAINER AND TRAINEE

Melanie made the same mistakes in parenting as she had in making life changes. First, she had the wrong goal. She wanted her son to serve her need to look good. But God wanted Melanie to train her son to serve Him (Deuteronomy 6:13).

Second, Melanie tried to change her child using her own strength (Isaiah 49:4). God wanted her to call on Him for help (Psalm 30:10).

Finally, she sought knowledge rather than wisdom. The Bible has nothing to say about potty chairs, targets, or prize charts. It doesn't offer toilet training in a day, but it does say, "Train a child in the way he should go, and when he is old he will not turn from it" (Proverbs 22:6). I am pleased to report that my now eleven-year-old child has been trained in the way he should go. To save him embarrassment, I want to explain that potty training is not a recent accomplishment! He is, however, continuing on the Bible's lifetime training program.

Toilet training is motivating for mothers weary of dirty diapers, but training of young superheroes should be motivating for all of us. Mothers or not, we are role models. When we are flying, boys and girls of all ages marvel at us and want to be just like us. When we take off the suit, park the plane, and let our inner brat run wild, children aren't just disappointed; they're scared.

Kids need heroes like they need vegetables and sleep. If we as mothers, grandmothers, aunts, teachers, and friends don't inspire them to look up, they'll look around to meet their need. Their peers will become their heroes. The problem with peer heroes is children, by their very nature, are fools (Jeremiah 4:22). Companions of fools suffer harm and we all suffer harm when children grow up to become adult fools. If we want our children to soar, we have to fly so they can look up to our example.

We must also train Incredible kids because training them trains us. Remember the fruit the Super Power can produce in us: love, joy, peace, patience, kindness, goodness, faithfulness, gentleness, and self-control? Children are like Miracle-Gro for spiritual fruit.

The love a child can grow in us is powerful. In *Ten Stupid Things Women Do to Mess up Their Lives,* Dr. Laura Schlessinger reports telling her husband that if she were in a boat and could only save him or her child from drowning, she would save him. After all, she reasoned, they could have more children together. After their first child was born, however, Dr. Laura asked her husband, "How well can you swim?"

You will grow in love when you spend time with children and you will grow in joy. Children's joy is contagious. I was emailed a video of a daddy making his quadruplet babies laugh and I watched it over and over again. I am still smiling thinking of their delightful giggles. Oprah, not a mother herself, brought Christmas gifts to the children of Africa and described her experience with them as joy that nearly overwhelmed her.

We will grow in love and joy and we will grow in peace when we work with children. A boy has been described as noise with dirt on it. I have noise and dirt times five. As a mother, I am so tempted to think longingly of a day when I will have a clean and quiet house. But my children are developing in me a clean and quiet heart. This peace enables me to cope with the noise and dirt in the world outside – noise and dirt that will always be there.

When we work with children, we also grow in patience. When women find out I homeschool, many mothers say, "I wouldn't have the patience for it." I tell them Melanie doesn't either, but I've learned it as I've taught. When my first child didn't understand something right away or didn't cooperate, Melanie would get so frustrated she would yell. And she was always in a hurry.

One morning I heard a mother in the YMCA's dressing room with her young daughter yelling, "Hurry! Hurry! Hurry up! Come on, let's go! We're in a hurry!" She kept up her impatient commands despite the fact her daughter seemed to be cooperating. I was horrified as I saw Melanie in that mother. I've learned being impatient with my children is like yelling at a tree to hurry up and bear fruit. Children grow on God's timetable and as we work with them, we will grow in patience.

When we work with children, we will grow in kindness, goodness, faithfulness, gentleness, and self-control. When I was a psychologist-in-training, I learned how to use biofeedback equipment to help those who have muscle tension and pain. We would attach electrodes to the patient's painful areas. Whenever the patient tightened the targeted muscles, a noise would let them know. As a result of this feedback, patients were able to keep their muscles relaxed, even in the face of stress, and avoid pain.

Kids make good biofeedback machines. When we're tense and lose control, children let us know. Sometimes they make some noise and other times they just reflect our bad behavior. When we work with children, we will grow fruit of the Spirit and avoid pain because biofeedback works.

WHAT TO TEACH

I'm often asked how I know what to teach in my homeschooling. The answer is books! The array of books, courses, and curriculums homeschoolers have to choose from is dizzying. Once the choice is made, however, the teaching is easy. You teach from the book.

If you're not a homeschooler or teacher, you probably don't teach children phonics, history, or science, but you do teach. We all teach children by how we live, often unintentionally. But we must also teach intentionally by the book – the same book that instructs us: the Bible.

Parents have a God-given responsibility to teach the Bible to their children that goes beyond sending them to church and Christian schools (Deuteronomy 11:19). Teaching the Bible must become a lifestyle – a part of our mornings, our evenings, our work, and our play. We can use the Bible for memorization, instruction, discipline, and even recreation.

My children and I memorize Bible verses together and study the basics of the Christian faith each morning. As we learn about science and history, we see what the Bible has to say. When the children disobey, we talk about the blessings and punishments the Bible associates with disobedience. In the evenings, we do family devotions or read biographies of Christian heroes who applied the Bible to their lives.

Parents ensure their children learn reading, writing, and arithmetic so they can have a good life – one filled with prosperity and leisure. Teaching our children the Bible is also to ensure a good life – the good life of knowing the Super Power. [29] We teach the Bible so our children will have the joy of knowing who God is and the privilege of knowing who they are.

My third son was unable to speak more than a few words until he was three years old. He was often frustrated in his desire to communicate, so he screamed. A lot. I gave him the nickname "Osama, Our Little Terrorist." He wasn't up on his current events, so I'm sure he wasn't offended, but I know he was affected. He seemed to scream even more when I joked. The names we give ourselves and others are powerful.

Biblical names, like Native American names, were descriptive. 1 Chronicles 4 gives a brief account of Jabez, a man named "Pain" because of his mother's difficult labor. I can't indict his mother for unkindness because I've referred to my children as pains, too! Well at least Melanie has. "Jabez cried out to the God of Israel, 'Oh, that you would bless me and enlarge my territory! Let your hand be with me, and keep me from harm so that I will be free from pain.' And God granted his request" (1 Chronicles 4:10).

No one wants to be saddled with a negative label. They're prophetic. That's why God has taken such care in labeling us. 1 Peter 2:9 says, "But you are a chosen people, a royal priesthood, a holy nation, a people belonging to God, that you may declare the praises of him who called you out of darkness into his wonderful light."

In the movie, *The Princess Diaries*, Mia Thermopolis learns she is not the average, awkward teenage girl she thinks she is; she is the Princess of Genovia. When the reality of her true identity becomes apparent under the tutelage of her grandmother, Mia changes. Because we Wonder Women are daughters of the King, our children are princes and princesses. When the reality of their true identity becomes apparent to them under our tutelage, they may change, too. I began calling my little screamer my "Spunky Kid" instead of Osama and he quieted down.

When we can say with confidence, "I am Wonder Woman!" we can confidently declare our children Inredible kids. With the Super Power, they may begin to act like them! Unfortunately, our children must contend with an inner brat just as we must. Like us, they do battle with the enemy daily. Instead of declaring war on these young Supers, however, we must commit ourselves to training them as allies. We can motivate their training by showing them the scars we bare for not wielding the sword of the Spirit and the bracelets of prayer. And like Helen in *The Incredibles* movie, we can remind our children never to forget who they really are.

LEARNING BY DOING

The *Konos* curriculum I use in teaching my children emphasizes hands-on learning. In the course of studying kings and castles, the children made tapestries, conducted a coronation ceremony, and created a giant cardboard castle. At the end of our unit of study, we hosted a medieval feast and dressed like lords and ladies. The children loved playing their parts and still beg me to repeat the unit so they can resume their royal identities. Your children don't have to wear costumes to be superheroes (although it helps!). What they need is a little hands-on training. Television, video games, and chat rooms cannot train our kids for greatness, but chores can.

Chores are any tasks that allow a child to learn adult responsibility and service to others. Chores teach character while they teach practical skills. Positive and negative consequences based on chores teach children the value of Incredible living. The key to successful chore training is not allowing your inner brat to be in charge of it. Brats beget brats, so make sure you are suited up as Wonder Woman to begin.

Chores must be taught in baby steps, FLYLady-style. To teach a child to fold laundry, for example, first teach him to sort clothing by item (e.g., shirts, shorts, socks/underwear). Then teach him to fold across and up using consistent language. Finally, teach him to put away. Show him, watch him, and then let him FLY. The Maxwells' Chore System described in *Managers of Their Chores* helps my distractible kids stay on course.

SEND YOUR ARROWS

As a mother of six young superheroes, I am often asked if I know "what causes that" – the babies that is. A father of eight I know answers the question this way: "Yes we do and we happen to enjoy it."

I do enjoy my children. They keep me laughing and they keep me humble. Melanie, on the other hand, finds children rather tedious. She often wishes they would leave her alone so she could do what she wants to do. She doesn't have time for training and thinks kids should do as she says, not as she does.

Have I mentioned that Melanie is a Fool? She doesn't realize that her children are a blessing from God – a means to defeat the enemy in the battle for change (Psalm 127:3-4). The Bible compares them to arrows. How many arrows do you want at hand when the enemy comes?

Even if you're convinced you cannot afford more arrows for your quiver, know that you cannot afford to neglect the arrows you have. Our old selves like to focus on an arrow's faults – its bent, its dullness, even the color of its feathers. Although a less-than-perfect arrow may miss its mark, we are still called to aim it carefully. Instead of arrow bashing, let's practice our marksmanship. None of our arrows will hit dead center because of sin. But one Incredible arrow can do some serious damage in the battle for change.

In *The Incredibles*, Bob and Helen thought it was safer to live as ordinary people. They were afraid to let their children be wonders. Their son Dash complained:

Dash: You always say 'Do your best', but you don't really mean it. Why can't I do the best that I can do?
Helen: Right now, honey, the world just wants us to fit in, and to fit in, we gotta be like everyone else.
Dash: But Dad always said our powers were nothing to be ashamed of, our powers made us special.
Helen: Everyone's special, Dash.
Dash: Which is another way of saying no one is.

Helen realized her mistake. She and her children had stopped living like the superheroes they were created to be. As a result, her marriage was a mess and her kids were sullen and disobedient. But when they assumed their true identities, something Incredible happened: they defeated the enemy and their lives were changed. With the Super Power, we can live that story line.

Epilogue:

Where to Go From Here

We have reached the end of our journey to Wonder Womanhood together and I am inspired! I am inspired because of what the Super Power has taught me with each page. I am inspired because if you have read this far, I know God has an incredible adventure in mind for you! I am inspired because I know this book is just the beginning of the good work God will bring to completion in both of us (Philippians 1:6).

I'm also concerned. I know you may have picked up this book in desperation. You may be:

With a boyfriend who's beating you
Addicted to drugs or alcohol
So overweight you can barely walk
Hopeless and suicidal
Ready to declare bankruptcy
Married to a man who doesn't "see" you
In a home so messy it could be condemned
A mother of a mentally ill child

If I had the privilege of sitting down with you to discuss your situation, I would listen, give you a hug, and maybe shed some tears with you. If we talked, I hope you would see my compassion for you and my desire to fight the battle alongside you. Without time face-to-face, I'm concerned you might think I'm offering a pie-in-the-sky answer to your pain. I'm not. You see, I don't believe this or any book will work for you, but I believe God will. I'm offering you the Help that's helped me. I'm showing you the light at the end of the tunnel. I'm pointing you toward the bright Morning Star (Revelation 22:16). Follow the Star, dear Sister, and you'll find your way home. Until you get there, I'll be praying for you.

I'm also concerned about Melanie. If you ever meet her, you won't be too impressed. She's self-centered, thoughtless, and disorganized. She's a hypocrite, a controlling wife, and an angry mother. I've known her all my life and trust me, she hasn't changed! Any errors you find in this book are most certainly her doing. If you do happen to meet Melanie, please accept my apologies in advance. I'm working on getting her under control.

Finally, I'm concerned about how you perceive me, Wonder Woman. Yes, I have a Ph.D., I homeschool six children, I help my Superman, I write and speak and I enjoy several hobbies. But there are lots of ways to be Wonder Woman! You can be Wonder Woman with no formal education, no children, no husband, and no hobbies. You aren't Wonder Woman because of what you do, but because of what the Super Power does through you. He gives each of us a different mission to fulfill, every one of them vitally important (Ephesians 2:10). If you're ready for your first assignment, begin the Wonder Woman Workouts that follow.

Now I must be off! The Super Power has a new mission for me and I can't wait to find out what it is.

Workouts for Wonder Women

The mythical Wonder Woman we know and love spent long days training in the use of the weapons and the power she'd been given. We, too, become the heroines we want to be by working out.

You can work out alone or with a group. Before you decide to work out alone, do you know someone who would like the support of a group in making life changes? People are busy these days and someone you ask may say no. But what if she says yes? She may be so grateful you took the trouble to ask her!

Place an ad in your church, work, or school newsletter asking if anyone would like to join you in a six-week book discussion on changing your life. Pray for respondents and I believe the right people will come. Have each participant purchase her own book or buy them in bulk and collect payment later. If you need to meet prior to reading the Introduction and first chapter, discuss your goals. Spend time getting to know each other and encourage members to come even if they don't complete the reading each time.

Groups may want to do two or three workouts at a time if meeting time is limited. If you're working out alone, take as much time as you need to finish each workout, but not so long that you lose your interest and motivation. If an "exercise" doesn't feel comfortable to you, don't do it. If you or your group wants to add your own exercises, by all means do so! Before doing any physical exercise, make sure you have a doctor's okay to begin.

Group or no group, if you're new to the Super Power, you will benefit from the mentoring of a mature Wonder Woman. She can function like a personal trainer who can help you accomplish more than you could accomplish working out alone. Most advanced Wonder Women would be honored to be asked to fulfill such an important role. If your mentor has never read the book, ask her to read it and do the workouts with you.

HOW TO DO THE EXERCISES

Each workout corresponds to a chapter in the book. You will want to read the chapters before doing the workouts. I've recommended music to go along with each workout. Music makes every job easier – especially the job of life change. However, music is a very personal art form. If you don't listen to the type of music I've listed, skip it completely, search for the lyrics of the songs online, or replace it with your own music. The Internet makes finding music and lyrics you like very easy. You may wish to make a CD of all the songs and listen to them in your group meetings.

The most important exercise is one that works the heart. Your heart will get a workout when you read, repeat, write, and reflect on the Bible verse provided. The warm-up questions are appropriate for personal reflection or group discussion. Share answers to Stretch questions only as you are comfortable. If you are a new Wonder Woman working out alone, choose the lightweight exercises. If you're a long-time Wonder Woman, the heavyweight exercises may be more challenging for you. A great heavyweight exercise is looking up the Scripture references in each chapter. If it's been a long time since you've "worked out" or you're short on time, choose the lightweight exercises. Do the Extra Workouts only if you are really inspired or if you are going through the book for a second or third time. Be sure to start and end your workouts with prayer.

The key to success as Wonder Woman is continuing to train. Perfection is not expected. If you do 80% to 90% of these exercises (or your own substitutions) and practice the principles behind them 80% to 90% of the time, you're on the Honor Roll! You will definitely see the life change you desire if you stick with it. I am praying for you and believing that God will grant you success!

Please keep me apprised of how God is using *So You're Not Wonder Woman?* in your life and group. Email me at melphd@aol.com and visit my Wonder Women blog at www.wonderwomen.typepad.com.

WORKOUT #1

HOME WORKOUT: Read Introduction and Chapter 1, "Wonder Years"

MUSIC: "Anyway" - Martina McBride

FOR THE HEART:
Many, O LORD my God, are the wonders you have done. The things you planned for us no one can recount to you; were I to speak and tell of them, they would be too many to declare (Psalm 40:5)

WARM-UP: Which of the following statements best describe you?

- ✓ Your house is such a mess that you begin to hyperventilate at the thought of having unannounced guests
- ✓ Your New Year's resolution is the same year after year
- ✓ One or more of your relationships is making you miserable
- ✓ You feel like life is out of control
- ✓ You're not the patient, firm, devoted mother you want to be
- ✓ You think you're lacking the willpower gene
- ✓ You forget things so often, your organized friends give you reminders without being asked
- ✓ You know you are your own worst enemy
- ✓ Life feels vaguely empty
- ✓ You've tried to change before and here you are…

What one change would you most like to make in the coming year?

STRETCH:
What dreams did you have as a Wonder Girl that remain unfulfilled?

What kinds of experiences made you doubt that you were Wonder Girl?

LIGHTWEIGHT:
Pray a bold and specific prayer for life change. Ask your group or another Wonder Woman to join you in that prayer.

HEAVYWEIGHT: Do the Lightweight exercise and then read Nehemiah chapters two through six and Proverbs 25:28. What should we expect as we work at rebuilding the walls?

EXTRA WORKOUT:
Read Sisterhood *of Faith: 365 Life-Changing Stories About Women Who Made a Difference* by Shirley Brosius as a daily devotional
Read *Gladys Aylward: The Adventure of a Lifetime* by Janet & Geoff Benge

WORKOUT #2

HOME WORKOUT: Read Chapter 2, "Who Do You Think You Are?"

MUSIC: "Wonder Woman Theme"

FOR THE HEART:
I praise you because I am fearfully and wonderfully made; your works are wonderful, I know that full well (Psalm 139:14)

WARM-UP:
Has anyone ever called you Wonder Woman? Have you referred to anyone else that way? What traits do people associate with the title?

Do you tend to set the bar too high or too low in your desire for change? Why is that?

STRETCH:
What does your old self/Flesh Woman/inner brat do that keeps you from believing you're Wonder Woman?

LIGHTWEIGHT:

Set the bar at just the right height this week for you to be challenged, but not overwhelmed. Record it here and ask your group or a girlfriend for an opinion on it.

HEAVYWEIGHT:

Do the Lightweight Workout and read John 4:1-42. If you were the woman at the well, what challenges to changing would you face? And what hope do you have? Who would Jesus say you are?

EXTRA WORKOUT:

Read *Having a Mary Spirit: Allowing God to Change Us From the Inside Out* by Joanna Weaver

Check out www.thebratfactor.com

WORKOUT #3

HOME WORKOUT: Read Chapter 3, "Wayward Years"

MUSIC: "The Real Me" – Natalie Grant

FOR THE HEART:
I have strayed like a lost sheep. Seek your servant, for I have not forgotten your commands (Psalm 119:176).

WARM-UP:
How does your old self compare to Melanie?

STRETCH:
Do you let people see the real you?

Do you have a secret that once revealed might free you to live as Wonder Woman?

LIGHTWEIGHT:
Pray for courage to be transparent with others. If you feel led, share the truth about the old you with your group or a trustworthy friend. If you need help with finances, see the resources, including the Mvelopes budgeting system, at www.crown.org.

HEAVYWEIGHT:
Do the Lightweight workout and read Genesis 38. Have you ever done something wrong to make a right change? Does your current behavior tell people who you really are?

EXTRA WORKOUT:
Read *Get Out of That Pit: Straight Talk About God's Deliverance* and *When Godly People Do Ungodly Things* by Beth Moore
Read *Chosen with a Mission* by Nancy Wilson

WORKOUT #4

HOME WORKOUT: Read Chapter 4, "Whirling Around"

MUSIC: "Jesus Take the Wheel" – Carrie Underwood

FOR THE HEART:
Repent, then, and turn to God, so that your sins may be wiped out, that times of refreshing may come from the Lord (Acts :19).

WARM-UP:
Have you ever gotten lost? If so, how did it happen?

Have you ever made a dramatic change in your life? What prompted the turnaround?

STRETCH:
What do you think would happen in your life if you let Jesus take the wheel?

What keeps you from getting out of the driver's seat?

LIGHTWEIGHT:
Pray, asking God to take over the driving. Tell Him you're sorry for all the wrong paths you've taken. Practice keeping the brat in the back quiet this week by listening to Christian music or Bible studies. The radio and Internet offer many free options.

HEAVYWEIGHT:
Do the Lightweight Workout and read Jonah, chapter 3.
The Ninevites' repentance was apparent in their behavior.
What would true repentance look like in your life?

EXTRA WORKOUT:
Read *It's Your Turn Now* by Debra Peppers
Read *God Allows U-Turns for Women: The Choices We Make
Change the Story of Our Life* by Allison Bottke and Cheryll
Hutchins

WORKOUT #5

HOME WORKOUT: Read Chapter 5, "Why It's So Hard to Change"

MUSIC: "Change" – Tracy Chapman

FOR THE HEART:
Trust in the Lord with all your heart and lean not on your own understanding (James 1:5).

WARM-UP:
When you want help with a problem, where do you usually look?

What life change have you sought the most knowledge about? How has your knowledge helped?

STRETCH:
When has leaning on your own understanding failed you?

LIGHTWEIGHT:
Seek the wise counsel of a Wonder Woman who has mastered the life change you seek. Practice the hard work of change this week by exercising and/or weight lifting. Remember to do a lightweight workout if you don't exercise regularly!

HEAVYWEIGHT: Do the Lightweight Workout and read Genesis 31:1-19. Despite Jacob's assurance that God was with them, Rachel takes her father's idols. What false gods are you hanging on to?

EXTRA WORKOUT:
Read *Weigh Down Diet* by Gwen Shamblin
Read *God's Power to Change Your Life* by Rick Warren

WORKOUT #6

HOME WORKOUT: Read Chapter 6, "Who We're Fighting"

MUSIC: "If You're Going Through Hell" - Rodney Atkins

FOR THE HEART:
Be self-controlled and alert. Your enemy the devil prowls around like a roaring lion looking for someone to devour (1 Peter 5:8)

WARM-UP:
Which of Wonder Woman's enemies do you battle the most (Perfection, Duke of Deception, Dr. Psycho, Dr. Poison, Hypnota, Devastation)?

STRETCH:
In what ways have you been aiding the enemy?

LIGHTWEIGHT:
Choose one means of defeating your primary enemy and practice it this week. Pray for victory!

HEAVYWEIGHT: Do the Lightweight Workout and read Exodus 17:8-15. The Israelites were immediately engaged in battle as they left the Desert of Sin. To win your battle from Sin, what will you have to do? How can you keep your hands raised to God at all times?

EXTRA WORKOUT:
Read *A Woman's Guide to Spiritual Warfare* by Quin Sherrer and Ruthanne Garlock
Listen to "Insight for Living" at www.insight.org

WORKOUT #7

HOME WORKOUT: Read Chapter 7, "What to Wear"

MUSIC: "Make Me Over" – Natalie Grant

FOR THE HEART:
…put on the new self, created to be like God in true righteousness and holiness (Ephesians 4:24)

WARM-UP:
Do you have an outfit you feel great in? Do you behave differently when you wear it?

STRETCH:
Which wardrobe rule do you dress without most often (belt of truth, breastplate of righteousness, feet of peace, shield of faith, helmet of salvation)?

LIGHTWEIGHT:
Remove any clothing from your closet not befitting a true Wonder Woman. Wear a favorite outfit this week and ask God for help in following one of His wardrobe rules. At the end of the week ask your group or someone close if they noticed your "new outfit."

HEAVYWEIGHT:

Do the Lightweight Workout and read Esther 2:1-17. Are you willing to take time to make yourself beautiful for your King? Read 1 Peter 3:4 and ask God to give you a makeover.

EXTRA WORKOUT:

Read *The Look* and *Lies Women Believe* by Nancy Leigh DeMoss

Read *Dinner with a Perfect Stranger* by David Gregory

WORKOUT #8

HOME WORKOUT: Read Chapter 8, "Weapons of Change"

MUSIC: "Pray" – CeCe Winans

FOR THE HEART:
The weapons we fight with are not the weapons of the world. On the contrary, they have divine power to demolish strongholds (2 Corinthians 10:4).

WARM-UP:
How would you characterize your Bible knowledge (preschool, elementary school, high school, college, or graduate school)?

Have you ever experienced a dramatic answer to prayer?

STRETCH:
Why aren't you using your weapons as much as you should to win the battle for change?

LIGHTWEIGHT:
Choose a Bible and an approach to prayer discussed in the chapter. Commit to making an appointment with the King every day for five minutes. Look up several verses that speak to the change you desire. Write them on index cards or sticky notes and put them where you'll see them all day (e.g., mirror, planner, computer, refrigerator, car dash). Say them as a prayer whenever you see them.

HEAVYWEIGHT:
Do the Lightweight Workout increasing your time as you feel led. Choose a new Bible and a new approach to prayer if your old one has become stagnant. Read 1 Samuel, chapter 1. Samuel's name was a living reminder of God's power through answered prayer. Choose a way to memorialize God's answers to your prayers (scrapbook, writing, audio/video taping, planting a tree, garden stone, etc.).

EXTRA WORKOUT:
Read *Let Prayer Change Your Life* by Becky Tirabassi
Read *George Mueller: The Guardian of Bristol's Orphans* by Janet & Geoff Benge

WORKOUT #9

HOME WORKOUT: Read Chapter 9, "Winging It"

MUSIC: "Because You Loved Me" - Celine Dion

FOR THE HEART:
But those who hope in the LORD will renew their strength. They will soar on wings like eagles; they will run and not grow weary, they will walk and not be faint (Isaiah 40:31).

WARM-UP:
What is your current evening routine?

Which of the routines described in the chapter (evening, morning, weekly, decluttering) is the most challenging for you?

STRETCH:
What clutter do you have that you've refused to let go of (including activities and relationships)?

LIGHTWEIGHT:
Shine your sink this evening and sign up for www.flylady.net's emails. Declutter for five minutes each day.

HEAVYWEIGHT: Do the Lightweight Workout, adding to your routines as you can. Increase time spent decluttering to fifteen minutes. Read Joshua 24:1-14. Who do the items in your home say you serve? Get rid of anything that keeps you from worshiping the Lord and having the victory you desire.

EXTRA WORKOUT:
Read *Sink Reflections* by Marla Cilley
Read *Managers of Their Homes: A Practical Guide to Daily Scheduling for Christian Home-school Families* by Steven & Teri Maxwell

WORKOUT #10

HOME WORKOUT: Read Chapter 10, "With Justice for All"

MUSIC: "Thank You for Being a Friend" – Andrew Gold

FOR THE HEART:
A man of many companions may come to ruin, but there is a friend who sticks closer than a brother (Proverbs 18:24).

WARM-UP:
What has been your experience with church?

How have friends been of help to you in changing in the past?

STRETCH:
Have you been a companion of Fools? How has it kept you from making the change you desire?

What keeps you from reaching out to other Wonder Sisters?

LIGHTWEIGHT:
Pray for your Fools and for the strength to pull up your emotional drawbridge. Plan to attend church this Sunday and look for a new Wonder Sister to join your league.

HEAVYWEIGHT:
Do the Lightweight Workout. If you already attend a church, consider how you might serve most effectively there. Pray about mentoring a new Wonder Woman or leading a group. Teaching is the best way to learn! Read the book of Ruth. Naomi failed to recognize the value of a true friend in her troubles. Do you have a Wonder Sister you've taken for granted? Write or call her to thank her for her love and faithfulness.

EXTRA WORKOUT:
Read *Fool-Proofing Your Life* by Jan Silvious
Read *Words Begin in Our* Hearts by Rhonda Webb

WORKOUT #11

HOME WORKOUT: Read Chapter 11, "Winning with Superman"

MUSIC: "Superman Theme"

FOR THE HEART:
For your Maker is your husband— the LORD Almighty is his name— the Holy One of Israel is your Redeemer; he is called the God of all the earth (Isaiah 54:5).

WARM-UP:
If you're single, do you agree it's possible to live happily forever after with or without Superman? Why or why not?

If you're married, what personality types do you think you and your husband are (Sanguine-Fun, Choleric-Control, Melancholy-Perfection, Phlegmatic-Peace)?

STRETCH:
Singles, if you knew you would never marry, how would you live differently today?

Married women, how are you trying to exert control in your marriage?

LIGHTWEIGHT:

Singles, make one change this week to live life happily ever after with or without Superman.

Married ladies, ask your Superman to tell you honestly if you are seeking to control him in any way. Pray for your husband daily and ask God for help in trusting Him to guide your husband.

HEAVYWEIGHT:

Do the Lightweight Workout. Married ladies, take one step toward living like Wonder Woman this week. Compliment your Superman daily. Read Proverbs 31:10-31. Does the way you live make your husband more respectable? How would the Proverbs 31 wife advise you if she knew you?

EXTRA WORKOUT:

Read *The Proper Care and Feeding of Husbands* by Laura Schlessinger

Read *Created to Be His Helpmeet* by Debi Pearl

WORKOUT #12

HOME WORKOUT: Read Chapter 12, "Working with Incredible Kids"

MUSIC: "In My Daughter's Eyes" – Martina McBride or "I've Been Watching You" – Rodney Atkins

FOR THE HEART:
Only be careful, and watch yourselves closely so that you do not forget the things your eyes have seen or let them slip from your heart as long as you live. Teach them to your children and to their children after them (Deuteronomy 4:9).

WARM-UP:
If you are not a mother, what opportunities do you have to inspire children?

If you are a mother, do you normally think of your kids as future superheroes? What hints of greatness do you see in them?

STRETCH:
If the children in your life grow up to be just like you, what will they be like?

LIGHTWEIGHT:
Talk with the children in your life about what God is teaching you. Tell them they are superheroes in the making. Begin praying for your children each day.

HEAVYWEIGHT: Do the Lightweight Workout and schedule time each week to teach your children God's Word. If you're married, include your husband in this time if he's willing. Read 1 Samuel 2:12-36. Do you care more for your children's favor than you do for the Lord's? How can you be careful to do through your children what is in God's heart and mind?

EXTRA WORKOUT:
Read *Managers of Their Chores* by Steven & Teri Maxwell
Listen to "Family Life Today" at www.familylife.com or "Focus on the Family" at www.family.org.

NOTES

1. *Just Thinking,* Spring 2007
2. Ben Patterson, "A Faith Like Mary's," *Preaching Today* Tape #87, transcript downloaded from PreachingTodSermons.com, 4. Quoted in *Having a Mary Spirit: Allowing God to Change Us from the Inside Out* (Colorado Springs: Waterbrook Press, 2006), 101.
3. Joanna Weaver, *Having a Mary Spirit: Allowing God to Change Us from the Inside Out* (Colorado Springs: Waterbrook Press, 2006), 101.
4. www.thebratfactor.com
5. Dictionary.com Unabridged v 1.1
6. Melanie Wilson, *Predicting Treatment Response Using the Stages of Change Scale: Application in a Clinical Drug Trial.* (Dissertation, University of Missouri-Columbia, 1995).
7. Easton's 1897 Bible Dictionary, www.christweb.com
8. www.12step.org
9. www.janicemcbride.com
10. www.praisemoves.com
11. Olivia & Kurt Brunner, *PlayStation Nation: Protect Your Child from Video Game Addiction*
12. *God's Amazing Book/Lesson 1: Looking Around: There is No Book Comparable.* (Reston, VA: Community Bible Study, 1990) 1.
13. www.answersingenesis.org
14. *God's Amazing Book/Lesson 4: Looking Backward: The Formation of the Bible* (Reston, VA: Community Bible Study, 1990) 4.

15. Becky Tirabassi, *Change Your Life Daily Bible*

16. Try www.biblegateway.com

17. www.pcmemlock.com

18. www.lwf.org

19. Janet & Geoff Benge, *George Mueller: The Guardian of Bristol's Orphans*

20. www.motherwise.org

21. www.lifeway.com/lby

22. www.savingdinner.com

23. www.nursesfonewborns.com

24. courtesy of *Starlog Magazine*

25. www.sweetmonday.com

26. www.classervices.com

27. Florence Littauer, *Personality Plus for Couples*

28. www.turningpointonline.org

29. R. C. Sproul, *When You Rise Up: A Covenantal Approach to Homeschooling*

For Speaking Engagements and Fundraisers for Wonder Women:

Contact Melanie Wilson, Ph.D.

melphd@aol.com
314-707-6510

927501

Made in the USA